COPING WITH DEATH

BOOKS DUE ON LATEST DATE STAMPED

AUG 7 1989
DEC 1 1 1989

NOV 1 3 1990
JUN 2 9 1991
AUG 2 8 1991
OCT 1 1 1991
NOV 6 1991
JUN 3 1992

DATE DUE

```
155
.937      Raab, Robert A.
              Coping with death. -- Rev. ed. -- New York :
          Rosen, 1989.
              135 p. -- (Coping)




              1. Death--Psychological aspects.  I. Title.
```

COPING WITH DEATH

DR. ROBERT A. RAAB

THE ROSEN PUBLISHING GROUP, Inc
New York

Published in 1978, 1983, 1989 by The Rosen Publishing Group, Inc.
29 East 21st Street, New York, N.Y. 10010

Copyright 1978, 1989 by Robert A. Raab

All rights reserved. No part of this book may be reproduced
in any form without written permission from the publisher,
except by a reviewer.

REVISED EDITION 1989

Library of Congress Cataloging in Publication Data

Raab, Robert.
  Coping with death.

  Includes index.
  Bibliography: p. 132
  1. Death—Psychological aspects. I. Title.
BF789.D4R3   155.9'37   77-2794
ISBN 0-8239-0960-3

Manufactured in the United States of America

Dedication

To my dear sister Joan of beloved memory.
We will never forget you. You are never far from our minds and hearts.
It is written: "The memory of the righteous shall be for a blessing."
And . . . to all those who have suffered the loss of a loved one and wondered "Why did it happen?"

"So teach us to number our days, that we may get us a heart of wisdom"
(Psalm 90:12)

About the Author

DR. ROBERT A. RAAB is the Rabbi of The Suburban Temple, Wantagh, New York. He also teaches in the Sociology Departments of Nassau Community College and Five Towns College.

A native of Cincinnati, Ohio, he received a B.A. degree from the University of Cincinnati and was ordained at The Hebrew-Union College Jewish Institute of Religion, where he earned the degree of Doctor of Hebrew Letters. His alma mater also awarded him the honorary degree of Doctor of Divinity. He has received training in Pastoral Counseling from the Post-Graduate Center for Mental Health, in New York City.

PHOTO BY MICHAEL ROSS

Before going to Wantagh, Dr. Raab was Assistant Rabbi at Temple Sholom, Chicago, and Rabbi of Temple B'nai Israel, McKeesport, Pennsylvania. He was also a military chaplain in the United States Air Force during the Korean War.

Dr. Raab is the author of *The Teenager and the New Morality*. He has also written for such periodicals as *American Judaism, Journal of the Central Conference of American Rabbis, The Jewish Spectator, The Jewish Criterion,* and the *Jewish Digest*. He is a past president of the Wantagh Clergy Council and of the Long Island Association of Reform Rabbis.

His wife, Dr. Marjorie Klein Raab, is Director of the Department of Program Planning and Development of Nassau Community College. They have two sons, Daniel and Joel.

Acknowledgments

Special appreciation to Ruth Rosen, whose wise counsel and encouragement enabled me to set down my thoughts about death. Her faith was a major factor in seeing this volume through to completion. Her enthusiasm never faltered during the long months of writing and reflection on this painful subject.

And gratitude to my dear wife, Margie, who knew that I could compose this book despite a very hectic, time-consuming daily schedule. Her belief in me makes everything possible!

Preface

Have you ever thought about death and dying? As a young person, your main concern is the life that is opening up before you. The possibilities seem endless. You dream dreams, you fantasize about your future. Yet as a teenager it is quite possible you have seen death. Perhaps you attended the funeral of a grandparent, and, seeing the anguish in your mother's eyes, you probably cried yourself. Or a young friend of yours was killed in an auto accident. You became numb. What could you say to the grieving parents? None of us is untouched by the experience of death.

When you were very small, you may have had a pet that died, and you buried it in the backyard. Death has a fascination as well as a terror. Violence and murder draw people to motion pictures. Plays and books often deal with the theme of death. Death is unseen, yet it lurks everywhere.

An ancient tradition says, "Enjoy life, for thou knowest not the day of thy death." This book is written to enlighten rather than to frighten. Hopefully, you will find fresh insights into an age-old problem.

ROBERT A. RAAB

Contents

I.	Why Are We Concerned With Death Today?	17
II.	Youthful Suicide	25
III.	Feelings We Cannot Control	42
IV.	Growing Old	52
V.	The Living Will	62
VI.	The Cost of Dying	73
VII.	Make Today Count	85
VIII.	The Child and Death	97
IX.	AIDS—What to Do?	110
X.	Religion's Answers	114
XI.	Conclusions	126
	Bibliography	132
	Index	133

COPING WITH DEATH

CHAPTER I

Why Are We Concerned with Death Today?

One might well ask, why such a concern with death? After all, our society is devoted to the idea of life. Advertising urges us to live for pleasure and fun. Cosmetics help to conceal our age, and in many ways our society places a great premium on being young. Why, then, in such a youth-oriented world, are we so concerned about death today?

The truth is that in growing up almost all of us have had or will have the experience of seeing a contemporary die. Funerals of young people are usually well attended, especially by their peers. Grief is seen on the faces of the young when a fellow teenager has been killed in an accident or dies of illness.

When we are young, we may have the notion that we will live forever. I was certain that by the time I grew up death would be conquered. Children have great faith in doctors. If we are sick, the doctor will give us medicine, and we will soon be well; the doctor will not let us die. Physicians are regarded as super-persons who will not let us down. Then, as we move through life, the older we get, the more we see others perish. It may be a grandparent or an uncle. One day they are with us, the next day we see the sad expression on our parents' faces, and before we know it, the funeral takes place.

Helplessness

In most areas youth has power. On the tennis court, we can fight hard to win. In class, we can strive to get better grades. If things are not going well at home, we may be able to find ways to communicate better with our parents and siblings. We have been taught that most problems can be solved by effort, combined with some brain and muscle power. And there is always a second chance. No situation is completely hopeless.

Such is not the case with death. If our pet dog is hit by a car and dies, we cannot restore her. If our cat dies of old age, we cannot bring him back to life. What can we do? Most parents can tell stories of their children's burying a pet in the backyard. My sons took a prayerbook and said prayers, after digging a hole to bury a small animal. The point is that most of us want to do *something* when death occurs.

If you visit a home where there is mourning, it is very difficult to know what to say. The children may well be your own age. What can you do? Everyone looks sad. There may be long embarrassing silences. A family member may tell the story of the death, with minute descriptions of the hour-by-hour events leading up to the end. We listen, perhaps horrified and fascinated at the same time. "She looked so well. She came through the operation beautifully. We brought her home. She was in remission. The doctor was so hopeful. Maybe we should have taken her to another doctor." The talk drones on.

What do you say to a classmate who has lost a parent? Words do not come easily. We put our arms around a friend. We walk and let her talk. We may not say very much, or there can be silence. Yet after a few moments the mourner says, "I feel so much better because you came over. It is good to have a friend like you." Your presence speaks louder than words. You did not have to utter a sound. Being there was sufficient.

Medical Attitudes

The medical profession is very much concerned with death. The doctor devotes his life to delaying its arrival; his training seeks to sustain life. The physician diagnoses the illness and treats it. Vast sums are expended, and hospital and medical costs rise precipitously.

The doctors are not of one mind on the advisability of postponing death. Some feel that every possible means should be employed to sustain life. Others hold that heroic measures through the use of sophisticated machines are too costly and only prolong the final agony. The Karen Ann Quinlan case is a dramatic example of this. She was kept alive on machines, even though her parents wished her to be taken off such drastic life-saving devices. Ultimately, after a legal battle, the court ruled that the family had a right not to permit the use of heroic means, and the machines were removed. She survives, still in a coma. Her case became front-page news. Doctors and lawyers expressed a variety of opinions. Some condemned the Quinlans for being callous and hard-hearted, while others applauded their honesty and their desire not to see their daughter endure further suffering.

Medical schools are now giving courses on the problems of death and dying. Greater sensitivity is needed. It is not enough for a physician to prolong life; there must be a reasonable prognosis that the life being saved has vitality. If the brain has been destroyed, merely keeping a patient breathing may mean a "living death." Also, it can leave psychological scars on the survivors, as well as subjecting them to enormous expense. It can become a serious problem. When do you take a person off the life-support machine? When do you put one on it? Is the decision to be made by the family or by the physician—or by both? Often there is a consultation between family and doctor, and a clergyperson may be consulted. The family may be loath to make the decision by themselves. However, if the patient has expressed himself, either verbally or in writing, the decision is easier. It is possible (while you are in good health), to write a statement requesting that heroic measures should not be employed to sustain you if you are stricken by an illness that appears to be fatal.

Sociology

The sociologist studies human behavior and seeks to gauge public attitudes. At one time taboos surrounded death, and it was spoken of in hushed voices. Today, however, death is "up front." From the time a child is small, he sees death on the television screen. In the 1960's, the entire nation watched the funeral of President John F. Kennedy. The assassinations of Robert Kennedy and the Rev. Martin Luther King were duly recorded and presented to television audiences. Marshall McLuhan, media expert and author of *The Media Is the Message,* holds that the media has a life of its own and has tremendous impact upon us. Television has turned the world into a global village. People are drawn closer together, since through satellite broadcasts we have instant knowledge. Wherever there are radios and television sets, we can be present simultaneously at important events. One sociologist has written that anything that is discussed or seen on television becomes an accepted part of our lifestyle. The attempted assassination of President Reagan was recorded on TV. More books appear on the subject. Euthanasia (sometimes called mercy killing) has been the focal point of numerous articles. The daily press runs articles about death and dying. Thanatology, the study of death, takes its place as a legitimate social-science concern. Sociologists probe to know how we really feel when death touches us. How sad are you? The psychologist may say that you cry at a funeral because you are afraid: if a contemporary can die, it can also happen to you. The young are especially afraid: "Of course I am afraid of death. I haven't really lived that long yet."

Newpaper articles cite the current death rate, noting that the rate currently continues to fall. Was it because people are living longer? Is medicine better able to sustain life? Is it a healthy statistic that fewer die if the survivors often live out their last years in poorly run nursing homes?

The Battle Against Aging

Modern society tends to look upon getting old as a sin. Previous generations honored the elderly, but today they are often seen as a nuisance. What shall we do with them as they enter the "golden years"? One oldster told me, "What is so golden about the golden years? All I have are aches and pains. I am just sitting around waiting to die."

Our society is built around what has been termed the Puritan or Protestant work ethic. A person's worth is determined by his job. If you do not work, you are useless. Work gives meaning to life. As earlier and earlier retirement ages are forced on the workers, we find persons in their vigorous fifties who suddenly are pensioned off. One day they are busy at their desks; the next day they are told to go fishing. Some doctors are convinced that early retirement leads to early death. For those not prepared for retirement, it can be a form of living death—a time without structure or purpose.

WHY ARE WE CONCERNED WITH DEATH TODAY?

When you are young, you seldom think about growing old. In your teens, vital tasks are life-related. Everything can be accomplished! As you move toward adulthood there are school, sports, parties, family chores, and many things to do. You are future-oriented. You discuss with friends what you want to do as your life's work. You may meet persons whom you admire. A history teacher may turn you on to a desire to become like her. An instructor in biology might stimulate you to think about becoming a doctor. Death is not something immanent; it is unreal. You may be well into your twenties and never have attended a funeral. If you are fortunate, death will not intrude; however, few escape.

No Taboos?

People are increasingly likely to discuss death. It is no longer a hush-hush subject, to be talked about while the young are out of the room. When President Kennedy died, his widow took her two young children to the funeral. Children watching this on television asked questions. Soon more and more of them said, "Why can't I go to a funeral?" Psychologists discussed the possible traumatic effects on children if they looked into a casket. Gradually something of a consensus was reached. A child should be allowed to participate in a funeral to the extent that he or she is emotionally ready to do so. If families are close and share good times, then they should also share difficult and tragic events. The accent, though, seems to be on the extent to which the child can emotionally absorb it. The parent who forces the child to kiss Grandma goodby in the casket may be doing the child great harm. Terrible nightmares and fright can result. Some persons are unable to enter a funeral parlor because of horrible experiences with death in their youth.

Death by Terrorism

We live in an age of terrorism, in which no one is really safe. On October 9, 1985, four terrorist hijackers seized the Italian luxury liner *Achille Lauro*. Taking the passengers hostage, they demanded that Israel free fifty imprisoned Palestinians. Among the passengers was Leon Klinghofer, a disabled sixty-nine-year-old New Yorker on a voyage with members of his family. Without provocation one of the hijackers shot and killed Klinghofer and dumped his body and his wheelchair overboard. Later the United Nations Security Council condemned this act of piracy as an "unjustifiable and criminal hijacking."

In the summer of 1988 a Greek tourist ship was attacked by terrorists and a number of passengers were killed.

It makes one wonder about the sanctity of human life in a world in which "revenge" is taken against the innocent in the name of some perverted idea of justice.

Not to be forgotten is the suicide attack by a terrorist who drove a TNT-loaded truck into the Marine compound at Beirut Airport in Lebanon. In the dawn of that October 23, 1983, 241 Marines and sailors, members of the multinational peacekeeping force, were killed and more than a hundred others were wounded. This shocking event ultimately resulted in the withdrawal of the American Marines from Beirut. Those who perpetrated this suicide mission believed they were part of a holy struggle to liberate Lebanon. Fanaticism, once again, caused the death of innocents. The driver of the truck no doubt considered himself a martyr, assured of a place in heaven. It was another tragic commentary on the times in which we live. Sudden death is always a possibility—be it in Beirut, on the high seas, or on the streets of our cities, where bystanders are gunned down as drug dealers shoot it out in their gang and drug wars.

Terrorist violence seems to flare up and then subside. But it always smolders beneath the surface. At one moment it appears as terrorists inflame the Palestinians on the West Bank of the Jordan River. At another moment terrorists take the life of a political prisoner when their "demands" are not met.

Someone has said that modern man lives always "on the edge." We are never sure what the next news broadcast will bring. Our generation is learning to live with the sudden death that comes in the guise of masked gunmen who are not afraid of the consequences of their actions. Terrorists may see themselves as taking risks in the spirit of altruistic suicide postulated by the French sociologist Émile Durkheim, going forth to battle for a noble cause. However, most of the world shudders at the acts of these fanatics. Death by terrorism is a tragic flaw in human society. Would that it were otherwise and that people might act out of compassion rather than revenge and terror.

The Atomic Bomb

The late Harry S. Truman was quoted as saying that he never had a sleepless night after he ordered the bombing of two Japanese cities. His action brought World War II to a swift conclusion. At the time Americans rejoiced that the war was ended. Today, however, moral judgments are pronounced. How could we actually drop atomic bombs on a civilian population? Guilt feelings are aroused. At the time the bombs were dropped, most Americans approved. Modern warfare had made death a matter of detachment. The pilot who pressed a button could not see the victims of the lethal missiles dislodged from his aircraft; thus, killing became a less personal matter. Also, if you killed in the name of your country, there was a patriotic aspect to your actions.

Years after the event, however, studies were made of those airmen who participated in the atomic raids on Japan. In many cases, they suffered psychological problems. It is quite possible that even "killing from a distance" can trigger emotional instability and breakdown.

Why Discuss Death?

So we are painfully aware that death is always before us. Each day we live, we draw closer to the reality of it. Along the path of life, persons we know will fall by the wayside. Deep in the unconscious is the knowledge that what happens to others must one day happen to us. This need not make us morbid and afraid. To be fearful of life can also be a kind of "living death." The person who lives life fully need not fear the final moment. And there may be some small comfort in the knowledge that when death comes to us, we make room for others to be born and to live out their "length of days" in this world.

Thought Questions

1. Have you experienced the death of a close friend? How did you feel about it?
2. Could you discuss the death of a friend?

3. Why do we feel so helpless when death strikes?
4. Is there such a thing as a "good" war?
5. Was it immoral of the United States to use atomic bombs against Japan?

CHAPTER II

Youthful Suicide

Most persons at one time or another have thought about taking their own life. Usually the idea remains only in our mind. Talking about it to others is a warning that we may be contemplating suicide at a conscious level. If a friend talks about suicide, do not take the matter lightly. It can be an indication of severe depression. The potential suicide is losing touch with reality, feels detached from the world, and sees death as an escape from problems.

Teenage suicide has been occurring at an accelerated rate. In 1960 it was reported that about 1,500 young people took their own lives, whereas in the 1980s it is estimated that more than 5,000 teens commit suicide each year. We hear of suicide pacts, with several teenagers locking themselves in a car with the motor running. Accidents and crime account for most deaths among teens, with suicide number three—and, it is predicted, soon liable to become number one.

Not Making It

Jean was the top student in a small high school in the Midwest. She was awarded every honor in school. She was popular, and all her friends predicted a brilliant future for her. Jean was flattered when an Ivy League university accepted her, but it soon became apparent that she could not keep up with her classmates. Jean had been the top student in a graduating class of 100. Her fellow collegians were outstanding students in classes of more than 1,000. She realized that her high school training had not been adequate, but she felt pressure to succeed so as not to disappoint her parents, family, and friends.

Jean was a victim of exaggerated expectations. Had she gone to the state university, the pressure might have been less. However, in the grinding demands and competitive atmosphere of this prestigious

Eastern university, Jean was out of her depth. She could not confide in her parents: what could she tell them? She had always been a straight A student; now she was lucky to get a C in most of her classes.

Her bright smile had faded. She had constant fits of depression. She took pills to stay awake all night to study. As a result, she was bleary-eyed in class the next day. Her classes had hundreds of students, and she was just part of the faceless mass in the giant lecture hall. Jean felt herself falling. No one was present to give her support. She had few friends to confide in, and the friends she did have were used to the "grind" of constant studying. They came from highly competitive high schools and had taken courses far in advance of normal high school requirements. The pressure became too much. The semester exams were a horror. She had spent sleepless nights trying to cram. Her mind was overtaxed. She went into the examination room in a state of physical and mental exhaustion. In her heart, she felt she was a failure. She waited with trembling hand to receive the results of the tests. When she saw her grades posted in the hall, she turned white. She had done even worse than she possibly could have imagined. What was she to do? How could the high school class valedictorian be on academic probation her first semester in college? How she wished she had gone to the state university, where so many of her friends were! They had written glowing letters of the fun they were having in college. What was Jean to do?

Tragically, there are many students—often from small towns—who matriculate in colleges for which they are not really prepared. They have been accustomed to success. Suddenly, they are faced with the possibility of failure. The "tough" colleges often have a sink-or-swim attitude. Failure or success is yours to achieve. If you do not measure up, how can you go home in disgrace? Small towns are like extended families; everyone knows everyone else's business. How can you cope with the inevitable questions about your failure? How can you walk down the street with a sense of pride and well-being? How can you face the reality of being asked to leave college because of academic failure? What course is open to you?

For the Jeans of this world, one of the options is suicide, a way to escape from problems. Jean may think, "This is the best way. I might as well end it all. I am a failure. There must be something wrong with me." In fact, of course, there is nothing wrong with Jean. She is the victim of the American drive for success. She was raised to believe that to fail is the greatest sin. Jean was a winner in life up to the age of eighteen. She was living in a teenage ivory tower. She had not yet competed in the post-high school world. Everyone had told her, from the time she was a little girl, that she was the brightest and the prettiest, and she had believed it. She was simply not prepared for the cold, ongoing demands of a college that was filled with valedictorians. She was in water over her head and told to sink or swim. She was sinking. She was not destined to be a survivor.

Studies have shown that a major cause of death in college student populations is suicide. It strikes down the serious student who simply cannot cope and cannot face failure. Sometimes a young person feels unable to go to anyone with the problem of failure and unable to forgive herself or himself. Suicide is a form of self-punishment.

What makes this doubly tragic in Jean's case is the fact that in all probability her parents would have listened and comforted her. Something within Jean prevented her from going home. The Jeans of our society are victims of the success syndrome. The college that accepted her did so because she came from a small town, and the authorities like to say that they have a wide geographic distribution in their student population. Also, she had done well in the small, limited educational system in which she was reared. Who is to blame? Is it the fault of society? Should we condemn the educational system that creates false and unreasonable expectations? Perhaps the parents are the villains. They praised Jean too much. Can we blame her teachers, who perhaps saw in her the fulfillment of their own dreams? Is the university that accepted her at fault? After all, it wants to have a "balanced" student body. Is it the fault of the college counselors and psychologists who did not notice Jean? She was loath to approach them with her problems, and she looked like any other freshman. She was intense, serious, and moved quickly from class to class. How was anyone to know what was going on inside her confused mind?

A Modern Tragedy

All of us—young and old—were truly horrified when we learned of the sudden death of Len Bias, age twenty-two. The day before that June morning in 1986 Bias had been the first pick of the Boston Celtics in the National Basketball Association draft. He was young, attractive, and talented. He was considered a role model for his contemporaries, a fine example of the best young American athletes. He died as he was celebrating his good fortune in his dormitory room at the University of Maryland. The probable cause of death: an overdose of cocaine. Upon hearing the news, Celtics star Larry Bird said, "It's horrible. I'm too shocked to respond. It's the cruelest thing I ever heard!"

The death of the six-foot-eight, 210-pound Bias truly shocked everyone. Cocaine can ruin even the finest and strongest of our youth. Today we have a new wave of deaths caused by the highly addictive drug crack, a cocaine derivative. Crack addicts seldom escape their addiction. Crack is cheap—and lethal.

Do drug abusers have a "death wish," or are they just foolish people trying to have "a good time"? Len Bias was partying on cocaine when he apparently took an overdose. The shock waves caused by his death are still vibrating through the minds of the young. If it could happen to Len Bias, it could happen to anyone.

We might ask whether Bias was a victim of the drug culture. Drugs are often considered fashionable. Frequently we read of athletes—amateur and professional—who are obliged to enter drug rehabilitation programs. Len Bias did not have the chance to be rehabilitated. He was taken too young. Some might say he was a victim of the life-style of our times.

Society and Suicide

Many years ago the French sociologist Émile Durkheim did a study of the types of suicides. Durkheim was not content with reading accounts of suicides; he wanted to know why people took their

---

[1] Pete Hamill column, New York *News,* Feb. 2, 1977.

own lives. He identified three categories: egoistic, altruistic, and anomic.

Egoistic suicide occurs when the self-esteem of the person is very low, and he or she lacks others who can give support and help. The alienated, lonely Jean would fall into this category. So would the teenage runaway who goes down to the "Village" and cannot find herself. Sociologists use the word *ego* to mean a person. We are all egos. Psychologists may see the word ego as descriptive of how we feel about ourselves. In common usage, if you have a damaged ego, it means you do not really like yourself. You may have feelings of inferiority, frustration, or guilt. It is not easy to function with a damaged ego. A person who constantly downs herself has little sense of self-worth. Unless you love yourself properly, it is difficult to relate to others. Psychologists are deeply concerned with self-worth. If you feel that you are valuable, you can function normally. An extreme example of this is the pretty girl who thinks she is ugly. Even though society sees her as being attractive, in her own eyes she looks terrible. A therapist would try to get her to see herself as the nice-looking person she really is. The doctor would try to find out why she has such a negative view of herself.

Durkheim's altruistic type of suicide puts honor and duty above everything else. Such persons are overly giving. They constantly risk their lives for a cause, and they may bring about needless death. Yet in their own eyes they are noble. The soldier who remains in the trenches firing at the enemy long after his commander has told him to retreat is—in effect—taking needless risk. The suicide battalions who throw themselves into the mouth of the enemy's cannon in a Kamikaze gesture are truly engaging in "altruistic" self-destruction. A stunt pilot or driver who takes unnecessary risks has a streak of "altruistic" suicide within his makeup.

Durkheim's third type of suicide, the anomic, is the person who has had a dramatic change of fortune with which he cannot cope. During the depression of the late 1920's and early 1930's, many businessmen suddenly went from tremendous wealth to a state of poverty as the value of their stocks and bonds tumbled in the great panic of the stock market. Such men could not face their families or themselves. They blamed themselves, and not the system. Durkheim was among the first to be aware that a society could be anomic —that is, that the society itself could be sick. He saw that social forces could drive distressed persons to take their own lives. Durkheim did not hold the individual alone to be responsible. Instead, he felt that poverty, social upheaval, aloneness, and alienation could drive one beyond the brink of normal action and reaction. For Durkheim, suicide was not just a breakdown of one's mental facilities. Instead, it had to do with the structure of a society that does not really care about individuals.

The Age of Rapid Change

Alvin Tofler, author of *Future Shock,* takes the position that in this world we are asked to absorb too much, too soon. In the process, the individual may suffer mental and emotional breakdown. He writes of the modern "throw-away" society: people are treated like objects; no one is important; people can be replaced. If Tofler is right, then suicides will increase. Some social scientists hold that in American society the machine is truly more valuable than the person. Instead of machines serving us, we serve them. The age of Stanley Kubrick's *2001*—when computers take over from man— will lead to a dehumanization of the world. Films and books give us science-fiction accounts of giant computers that will ultimately enslave mankind.

Marshall McLuhan says that our lives are dominated by television. This breeds a world of instant success, followed by instant failure. Where are the hit musical records of six months ago? What happens to the musical and film stars of a few seasons past? Television has a tremendous appetite. It gobbles up people. It hungers for the new fresh face, song, and idea. Overexposure on television can hurt an actor or a politician. In political campaigns there is always the fear of either too much exposure or too little. We live in times when visual images impress themselves on the mind. Today no one knows you. Tomorrow you are known because you appeared on a national network talk show.

More and more we hear of the problem of "instability." A person who is not stable is not in touch with reality at a good working level.

Tofler holds that we experience too much change too rapidly.

Nothing seems to be permanent. In an earlier age, a child would hold on to a Raggedy Ann doll, and it would be handed down to her daughter. Precious heirlooms in the family would go from one generation to the next. There was a sense of importance about the things we owned. Currently there seems to be a fad for nostalgia and for the dress, styles, and objects of days gone by. America's Bicentennial celebration probably heightened this fascination with the past —all at once, history became fashionable.

In the long run, however, what is new is considered best. As we discard yesterday's newspaper, we often do the same thing with today's friendships. Relationships are fragile in a world on the go, in which every year one of every seven Americans moves to a new location. The moving companies are a major industry in the United States. No sooner do we put down fragile roots than the family is forced to move because father has a better job offer elsewhere. Economic recession can even speed up this process, as a desperate search for jobs takes place. The young person graduating from high school or college may find that a job is not to be had in his hometown. Young men and women entering the field of teaching are not likely to find employment in their home communities. The link holding relationships together is often the telephone, as our mobile society keeps us on the go. It may be that the wheel and the clover-leaf pattern of the superhighway is the new symbol of our age.

Tofler pointed out that Raggedy-Ann has been replaced by the trade-in doll. When a child gets tired of her doll, she can trade it in on a newer model. There is even a doll on the market that, when you twist its arms, "grows up," becoming endowed with adult characteristics. What can one say of such a world? It breeds anomie. It may give us all a touch of autism, a state of absorption in fantasy and consequent lack of touch with reality.

David Riesman wrote of *The Lonely Crowd*. In a big city one can be very much alone. He held that the larger the city, the more likely people are to be afraid of one another. If we walk the streets of a large city, we cannot simply smile and say hello. We fear the stranger. We put multiple locks on our doors. In major cities, residents are afraid to take a short stroll in the evening. Even in "safe" suburban areas, people often keep large dogs for protection. The crime rate rises. Accounts of brutal murders, rapes, and kidnappings occupy the front pages of newspapers. We live in a time of instability and fear. If life is seen as cheap and disposable, some may become hardened to the death of others. Because of the communications "overload" whereby we hear of so much death, we tend to become immune to it; death loses its impact. Today's tragedy is replaced by an even worse one tomorrow. In such a world the person does not count. When life is cheap, who can get excited about a death, unless it occurs within your own small circle of family and friends?

Living with Stress

Sociologists study the effects of stress on all age groups. They have discovered that certain groups are particularly victimized by society. Suicide rates are especially high among young black men in their twenties and adolescent black and white girls.

It has been pointed out that black children often have special problems. Many of them live in a matriarchal society, where the father is seldom present. Thus the young black male does not have a good male model with which to identify. He may be one of a large family, in which his mother has precious little time to devote to him. Caught up in the struggle just to exist, the young black male may turn to his peers for emotional support. His choice of companions may not be the best. Living in a society in which his peers are in gangs, stealing tires, then—to win acceptance—he is likely to join the gang. If his mother lacks the strength to give him direction and his choices are limited, he may well fall in with the wrong type of companions.

Every adolescent has a tremendous need to be accepted. We do not live alone. We need friends, to help us discover who we are and to aid us to develop our own value system. While the young black male may lack a good male image with which to identify, his sister suffers the same lack. She may have less tendency to suicide, however, since she can identify with the female head of the household.

If one lives with despair and one's defenses are down, then suicide may occur. Every so often we read of a jail inmate who hangs himself. Prisons seldom rehabilitate; they tend, rather, to turn out hardened criminals. Tragically, the jails do not serve their intended function. Society does not forgive the convicted person; he or she is considered to be a criminal forever. With few avenues open back into society, it is no wonder that the convict, with a wounded ego, goes with those who share his life experience.

Why is suicide increasing among young women? Some sociologists believe it results from the changing role of the female in our society. In the past, females were reared to be submissive and quiet. Girls were not supposed to be aggressive, but rather "ladylike." Today, ideas are changing. In preschool nurseries, girls can be rough-and-tumble as well as the boys. Public schools offer vocational training for girls. Even as the male can learn home economics, the female can learn carpentry and the mastery of the slide rule. Girls and boys wear blue jeans as the standard uniform of the teenager. The hair length of males and females may be pretty much the same. The concept of being "feminine" is challenged. The helpless female of the past is replaced by the aggressive woman of today.

Girls need no longer fear being considered smarter than boys. A girl can take on a boy at tennis and not feel she has to lose so as to protect her partner's feelings of masculinity. Males today can cry. Girls can use bad language. We are not so easily shocked as we once were.

In a new age, we find the female subjected to new strain and stress. If you are raised to be demure, soft, sweet, and cuddly, what happens to you when there are fewer males who want a clinging, dependent woman? I have found in my sociology classes in college that males welcome as wives women who work and command excellent salaries. Many youths of college age welcome the idea of not being the sole breadwinner in the family. They feel that some of the pressure on them is thereby reduced. At the same time, many girls are not prepared to assume a role that they have not been adequately socialized to undertake, and the social system has not yet become fully reorganized.

The new woman must compete in a world often dominated by men. In her old role, she knew her place as wife and mother. Today, she goes into the arena of the business world, or of politics, fully aware that she has to compete. She is often at a disadvantage. Can she use her feminine wiles? Must she submit to the sexual advances of her boss in order to rise on the corporate ladder? She is still a female, and the males do not easily welcome the new competitor.

Women often complain that their rise in the work force is limited. Seldom do they become the top executive of a firm. When promotion time comes, it is usually a panel of males that decides who shall move up. Being female is not a help in the competitive society of today. Some can live with stress better than others.

Our society is geared to success. We are socialized to live above our means in a credit-card civilization. This premium on getting ahead wreaks its havoc upon both the females and the males. Not only does the female suffer role strain, but the male also has new adjustments to make. Where formerly the male competed only with fellow males, he now must fend off the aggressive woman who seeks to advance, possibly at his expense.

When the male goes to a job interview, he seldom finds himself competing strictly with other males. He may even find that some employers are giving preferential treatment to females, who are often classified as an oppressed minority. So the male is not without his ego problems. He, too, may be terribly frustrated if women are "getting ahead" of him in his career goals. If he has to submit to a woman boss, his ego may not be able to stand such a strain.

A generation ago, the male was reared to be the aggressor. His main role was to grow up and be the breadwinner of a family. To be masculine meant to excel in sports, to be willing to fight to defend oneself, and never to be a sissy. The sissy was interested in cooking, classical music, theater, and ballet. To be called a sissy was to receive a terrible label. It meant you were not one of the gang. Little boys were expected to roughhouse and get dirty, to be sloppy, to push and shove. If a boy is shy and bookish, his parents worry. Even today, if he is attracted to the arts, there is the fear that he has homosexual tendencies. There is still a strong streak of machismo in our society. Males do not easily move into new roles.

The young male today is changing, however. To help with housework and with the new baby is not considered unmasculine. On the other hand, if the young male carries his girlfriend's purse when out walking, others may stare at him. The male is somewhat unsure. Should he pay for the girl's ticket to a movie? Should he open the door for her as they enter a building? Must he walk on the outside, nearest the street, when they are out for a stroll? Does being attentive, opening doors, lighting cigarettes still have some social significance? Should he stand and give his seat to a female on a crowded train? Social mores and customs are undergoing change. With the blue-jean generation, more and more quality of attitude develops. What is distinctly masculine or feminine anymore?

Role Strain

In the 1920's men jumped out of windows because the stock market crashed. In the 1980's is it possible that role strain will lead to thoughts of suicide? More and more we hear the words, "I cannot cope. I do not understand what is expected of me." Males are also under greater pressure to perform sexually. In an earlier age, less stress was placed upon sex. It was a natural function that followed marriage. The young couple were expected to learn from each other. Today, our world is highly sexually oriented. The male is expected to be proficient, and the same can be said, to some extent, of the female. Rising demands and expectations may be too much for the new American male, now emerging from his teenage years. Some psychologists see an increase in impotence among young men. They attribute this at least in part to the inability of the male to know what it means to be a man. What is virility? What is a real man?

One sociologist has said that the John Wayne image is what is ruining the American male. He may have tried, in the past, to be too masculine. Now, he can no longer be the strong silent type. Society wants him to be verbal and expressive. But he may not be able to cry, even at a funeral. He was taught as a child that boys do not cry; they just grin and bear it—keep a stiff upper lip.

Now, society changes. Under the impact of the women's liberation movement, there is talk of men's liberation. The man is now free. But free for what? His old accustomed, comfortable role is gone. What is to replace it? He may be uncomfortable, feeling that he does not "fit in." In one of my classes, when we were discussing the male role, a student reminded the class that putting down new flooring and taking care of the lawn were also forms of housework. What he was saying is that if a man does not wish to do the dishes or start the dinner, he can do many other things around the house, and he should not be condemned if—for example—he is awkward about changing the baby's diapers.

Psychology has taught us that it is very important to have a sense of self. We must feel that we are worthy. At the same time, we should know what our role or roles in life are likely to be. We are living in a time of transition. Definitions of male and female are being modified and changed. Society itself is not certain what is appropriate behavior. What was forbidden yesterday is approved today. Television has a tremendous impact. There is much openness. Permissiveness is equated with a new maturity. What roots do you have as a young person today? Do you know who you are?

While the military draft was in effect, the typical American male spent two years in uniform. He finished high school and went into the army. During that time, he could resolve his identity crisis, if he had one. While much has been said against the draft, it did afford the male the chance to be away from school and to face some of the real problems of life. With the end of the draft, I have noticed that some males have what can only be called "book-learning" fatigue. They need to take off from their studies for a year or two. Constant testing and the pressure to get good grades can take their toll—on males and females as well.

Society values the white-collar worker. Young people are reared to believe that they must go to college to amount to anything. At the same time, colleges can no longer guarantee jobs for the graduate. There can be a loss of self-esteem if one prepares for a career and there are no positions. This generation is not facing war on a battlefield in Asia. It is confronting the battle of economic survival, but this is also a struggle that takes its toll. If the suicide rate is rising among the young, it is understandable. In a competitive, mobile world where much is demanded of the young, not all will "make it." And if role strain and conflict are added to all the other problems, it is no wonder that the confused young person—male or female—may not really know who he or she is.

If you do not know who you are, then the life force—the drive to do and to achieve—may fail. A person in our society cannot just exist. We live by the Puritan work ethic. We must be productive and know who and what we are. When the psychological and social props that support us begin to fall away, chaos can result. If one is sufficiently disoriented, then thoughts of suicide can come to mind.

To Die Young?

Adolescence is a time of experimentation. Surveys indicate that at least 40 percent of the adolescents in America experiment with drugs. To take an overdose can be either accidental or purposeful. It is tragic that "ups" and "downs" are so readily available. The young person is tempted to experiment. He or she may get so far into the drug scene, that severe depression may set in. When one is very much "down," suicidal thoughts emerge. Young people generally are subject to wide swings on the emotional scale. At one moment they may be singing and full of energy and a few minutes later plunged into sadness. The coroner's report on the tragic death of actor John Belushi indicated a heavy overdose of drugs.

If you are in the mood to think "What's the use?" or "The world would be better off without me," you reveal a poor self-image. This feeling may be traced to difficult childhood experiences. Some psychologists might feel that you had suffered an absence of love. The teenager who must constantly be in the spotlight may well be a person who was ignored by parents and family as a child. If one is rejected by society, deep despair can set in. Illness can be real or imaginary. A troubled mind can be even more worrisome than a broken leg. The leg will mend: the results are visible. The mind that is sick cannot always be detected. It is possible that in your peer group there are persons who are thinking about suicide. They may be more depressed than you or their parents realize. If a friend talks frequently about suicide, the family should be alerted. Never take lightly any person's talking about self-destruction. The very act of verbalization is a danger signal. The youth who says "I might as well be dead" is really giving a signal. He is saying, "I need help." The potential suicide is saying, "Please do something. I am desperate." Too often when someone talks this way we say, "Aw, you're only kidding. You can't be serious. Buck up, things will get better." Such words of encouragement are seldom effective. To the depressed person, we seem to be saying, "What you have is not serious. Forget it. It will go away." Tragically, such thoughts may not disappear. Freud said that deep within us is a force called the *id,* which can push us toward life, or toward the death instinct, which he called *thanatos*. Many psychologists hold that the life and death forces are in constant battle within each of us. For most of us in the normal range, the life force is winning. For others, filled with rage, anger, and frustration, the death wish may be coming forth to dominate. Thus, if we talk about suicide, it is the way our conscious mind is telling us that one of the viable options is to take our own life.

The youthful suicide is looking for a permanent escape from terrible problems. He or she feels that there is no answer. Suicide is a way to avoid responsibilities. If you are dead, there is no need to make decisions. Nothing more is required of you, no further demands can be made.

In the 1980s we are seeing an increasing number of suicides among victims of AIDS (acquired immunodeficiency syndrome). This lethal disease primarily afflicts homosexuals and intravenous drug abusers. At first limited in scope, it has spread so that no part of America is entirely free. No cure is known. Is it any wonder that the AIDS patient, often scorned and avoided by family and friends, entertains thoughts of suicide? Even when the family is supportive, the patient may not wish to be a burden to loved ones. Living without hope, the AIDS patient can easily become depressed and resort to suicide.

Who Owns You?

Society teaches that we are free. Situation ethics holds that in life we should not be governed by preconditions. We should approach each new situation with a fresh perspective. Do not be fettered to the ideas of the past. Situation ethics can certainly cause trouble in the area of suicide prevention. If you are a totally free agent, who is to say that your life does not belong to you? Religion teaches that no person has the right to kill himself, that suicide is a type of murder. Ironically, some states have laws making it a crime for a person to take his own life.

Freedom involves responsibility. Some psychologists hold that many persons are self-centered, thinking only about what is good for them, rather than what they owe to others. If you are wrapped up solely in your own concerns, it is possible that this total immersion in "what is good for me" may lead to the thought, "I am in complete control of my life—as well as my death." The narcissist (the term for one who is totally concerned with himself) sees the world in terms of how it serves him. If the world exists to serve him, and he is not happy, then such a person might decide to end it all. In doing so, he exercises control over his immediate environment.

Frustrations of the Other-directed Person

It is possible for a young person to be very idealistic, but the idealist soon finds many frustrations. The world is not decent. People can be deceitful. So the altruistic suicide gives way to despair. The young child who is raised with loving parents develops the belief that the world is loving; however, experience shows that this is not true. The teenager may confront hostility and meet persons who are not as loving as his family.

It is good to be raised with affection. If we have poor mothering, we may develop a negative self-image. However, it must also be pointed out that the sensitive, totally idealistic young person cannot always stand the strain of living in the pragmatic, real world. The boss at your part-time job is a tyrant, making unreasonable demands. You encounter a teacher in school who treats you unfairly. People you thought to be friends can betray you. In ways both large and small, we soon discover that the world is not exclusively a friendly place. Seeing this, we may be motivated to change things. Young people tend to be idealistic. You may feel that all problems can be solved if there is goodwill on both sides. But there can be an absence of goodwill. In Ireland, Iran, and Lebanon, to name only three places, there can be wars between essentially decent people. Even Peace Corps volunteers have encountered resistance to their efforts. The point is that we are imperfect persons, living in a world that is far from perfect. Because of this, there is frustration.

If one becomes totally impatient, one can give way to despair. As a young person, you want to help, but people reject your outstretched hand. You see what they should be doing but they do not see things as you see them. You wish to reach out and touch them, and give them love; they reject and mock your advances. You begin to wonder, "What is wrong with me? I was taught that it is important to help my fellowmen, yet they do not want my help. Why do they resent me? Maybe there is something wrong with me?" Out of such desperate feelings of despair may arise the death wish. "Since I cannot make the world better, I am a failure. Since I am a failure, I do not deserve to live. The fault is with me. I can resolve the conflict, by removing myself from the struggles of life in this world." If one is rebuffed often enough, suicidal thoughts can arise. Psychologists say that most people, at some time in their lives, think about suicide; but the majority do not dwell morbidly on the topic. They think about it for a while, then go on to other matters. It does not consume them. The danger is when you become obsessed with the thought of suicide; then it becomes like a devil within you, taking control.

Psychologists might say that your id is out of control, and your ego and superego (conscience) cannot direct the id into constructive channels. For Freudians and others, the death wish is always buried deep in the unconscious. Most can cope with life. Most can "bounce back" after a period of feeling blue. For most teenagers, despair does not linger. It is quickly replaced with good feelings. If you find yourself fantasizing about taking your own life, it is important to discuss these thoughts with your family and your doctor. Probably it is nothing to be concerned about, but it might be good to talk about your feelings to someone. Sharing thoughts can often relieve tensions.

On the Brighter Side

In actual fact, your chances of being a suicide are very small. Less than 1 percent in the teenage category are destined to take their own life. But for that minority the problem can be pressing. There are suicide or crisis "hotlines" in most cities, through which the depressed person can call and talk to someone if he has no one at home with whom to communicate. Relief of anxiety is important. Just talking to friends can be helpful. You may wish to contact your family clergyperson. Many avenues of help exist if suicidal notions persist.

Youth is a period of change and challenge. Most young people are flexible enough to rebound from disappointments. We learn rather early in life the limits of actions. We live in a world of prescribed possibilities. This does not mean that we should curb our impulses to improve society. We cannot live in a private shell and reject the world. The very sociology of our lives demands that we be participants and not spectators, and in the act of participating and reacting, we learn how to work with others. The mature young person begins to understand that life involves give and take. We cannot always have things our own way. We are not all-powerful. Psychologists have a term for this: the Messiah complex. Some people feel that they can do anything, but life does not work that way. We are humans, living in a world that cries out for us to do our best. The world is perfectible. Setbacks are part of life, but we strive not to be defeated by obstacles. Often the stumbling block is buried somewhere deep inside of ourselves. If the problems become overwhelming, it is not a sign of weakness to seek aid. Rather, the person who seeks help is showing maturity, vision, and wisdom.

Thought Questions

1. Have you ever thought about suicide?
2. Do you think it is possible for a student to become so depressed that he or she would commit suicide?
3. Is the world changing so fast and creating so many pressures that we may see more suicides in the future?
4. How can you remain calm and in control with the society in such turmoil?
5. What is meant by "role strain"? Why can this lead to suicide?
6. Do you believe there is such a thing as an "identity crisis"?
7. Do you know who you truly are?

CHAPTER III

Feelings We Cannot Control

Often we cannot understand our own behavior. Such a problem can plague us at any age. You may ask, "Why do I suddenly cry for no apparent reason?" Or, "Why do I suddenly think of someone who has died?" "Why does the thought of my dead grandfather make me feel so sad?" "Why do I become irritable on the anniversary of the death of a loved one?" You may even question your own sanity. You may wonder why the dead have such a hold on the living. The person is gone, yet, he or she is still very much a part of your life. If a marvelous teacher in school is suddenly killed in an accident, there can be an awful sense of shock and helplessness. When a young person dies, the shock may be almost unbearable. The confused faces of teenagers at a contemporary's funeral are very obvious. In your mind is the eternal "why." The "how" of most deaths is known; one dies of an illness or an accident. The "why" remains elusive, and because of this we may feel an inner rage. We would like to know why we react to death as we do. Yet even the most rational of us may experience feelings that are difficult to categorize.

Psychologists are engaged in the study of reaction to death. Dr. Elisabeth Kubler-Ross provides some useful guidelines, distilled from many years of work with the dying and their families. She has categorized the usual stages a person goes through on seeing someone dying. The stages may not occur in exactly the order that Kubler-Ross indicates them; yet she seems to feel that one or more of the reactions do occur. They are reflected in both the patient and the survivors.

Denial

The first stage can be denial. You do not want to recognize that this is happening to someone you love. You think, "It could not be that my friend is stricken. Of all the people in the world, it cannot be someone I care about so much." The act of denial means that we push the idea out of our head as absurd, ludicrous, something that cannot be happening to someone we know. Teenagers may go through the adolescent years and never see death. Your parents are probably fairly young. Unless an aged grandparent dies, you may move through the teen years relatively unscathed. You read about death in the paper, but that does not directly affect you. You may be moved to tears by a television show to raise money for multiple sclerosis. You see a crippled child on the screen; it is sad, but the child is not your sister. When a famous person dies, you see mourners coming out of the church or synagogue. You are interested but not deeply touched.

A loved one is stricken. There are hurried phone calls. The sound of an ambulance pulling up to the house may assault your senses. The dying person gasps and struggles to live. You may even be the one to administer mouth-to-mouth resuscitation if the victim needs it. Closeness to the victim causes many feelings to erupt. Thoughts are uncontrollable. In the midst of trying to revive a stricken person, you may wonder, "What am I doing here? Can this be my grandfather who has keeled over? We were just sitting and talking; now, suddenly he has passed out." Fear grips the heart. Denial is an expected reaction. It is a defense against reality. If we deny that something takes place, we are shoving it into the back of our minds. Reality does not please us, so we invent a different reality.

Denial need not be bad. It may even free us to act. We may be functioning as if in a dream. We go through certain motions, carried along by events. Yet we deny—deep down—that they are real. When a bereaved parent says, "I know that one day my son will walk through that door," then that parent is denying the child's death. One parent said, "If I were ever to stop believing that someday my child will return, then I would fall apart." Denial can be a defense against reality. The person may need the prop of denial to function. Were the parent honestly to face the fact that her child has died, she might truly crumble into deep depression. The wise psychiatrist is very careful about robbing patients of their defenses. Unless you can replace such defenses with an adequate substitute, caution is advised. It may be necessary to deny a reality that you are not ready to acknowledge. Denial, then, has its uses. It gives us time to readjust our thoughts. Do not feel that there is something wrong with you if, upon hearing of the death of a loved one, you say, "Oh, no. That simply cannot be true." Your reaction is perfectly in accord with the normal response of most of us when we hear of a death. Do not be afraid to express your denial openly. Your experience is certainly within the normal range of reactions.

Anger

Kubler-Ross lists the second stage as that of anger. You may become very angry with the doctors. Why did they come so late? Why were they not able to revive the stricken one? Why did the medicines fail to work? Why was the operation a success, but a few days later the patient died? You may also become enraged with yourself. Why wasn't I home when my father was stricken?

You may also direct your feelings at God. You might say, "If God is good, and my grandmother was good, why did she have to die?" Of course, you know that everyone has to die, unless we unlock the secrets of immortality. You are angry with an unfeeling God. If God really cared about you, He would not have taken grandfather away. Rage bubbles up. Again, there is the feeling of frustration. You are helpless. You cannot fight against death. You talk to God, but he does not answer. The doctors give you their sympathy; they tried the best they could. Your clergyperson may tell you that the dead have gone to a better world. Well-meaning friends may say, "It is God's will." You cannot understand how it could be God's will when a school friend is killed in an automobile accident. The person was good. She never hurt anyone. Why her, of all people? Friends say, "People are dying every day. Someone has to die." This is not very comforting. Why should *my* friend die? Anger does not diminish, but you really are not sure where to direct it. Lynn Caine in her book *Widow* tells how she became angry at her dead husband. She felt he had deserted her and left her alone to raise the children. In her anger, she felt that he had copped out on her. She did not want to be angry with him, yet she was. She could not control her feelings.

You may subconsciously be angry at the dead. You feel that they have left you. Your anger can take many strange forms. It can be, as Lynn Caine says, a type of "craziness." The survivors may do strange things and have "shameful" thoughts. If you disliked the dead person, it can also create a problem. A young child who thinks, "I wish she was dead," and then the person actually dies, may be consumed with guilt. She thinks that her wish actually caused the death of her friend. If she was angry with her father and then he dies a day later, this can be very destructive. We know our thoughts do not have the power to kill, yet we feel guilty because we had such negative ideas. Anger is a very human emotion. Its roots can be in feelings of rage, helplessness, and guilt.

Bargaining

When one we love is dying, we may wish to make a deal with God. You say, "God, if you give grandmother a few more years, I promise that I will be a good person. I will never do anything wrong." Your parents might think, "God, if you let my child live, I will give 10 percent of my income to the church or synagogue." One of our defenses against facing the reality of death is to think that we can buy God's pardon. Or we may feel that if we pray unusually long, death can be avoided. Our prayer is a monologue; we may talk to God, but He does not answer. This can lead to a repeat of stage two, which is anger. We become enraged because there is no one with whom to enter into a contract. Our lives are built around exchanges. If I do something for you, then you are in my debt. Parents often make deals with their children: if you take out the trash and do the dishes, you are allowed to use the car. In the world of human beings, we constantly obligate others to us. And, when we do someone a favor, we expect a reward in return. If I invite you to dinner, I expect to be invited to your home later. But, if that return invitation never comes, you are not likely to be invited again.

In life, a certain number of such "exchanges" are necessary. There are many contractual arrangements. In the business world, we sign a contract and are then expected to deliver the merchandise or service. Employees contract themselves out to employers; their wages are the result of the agreement.

When death threatens, there is no way to enter into a contract with God or with the doctors. No human or superhuman power can provide a document to guarantee additional days or years of life. Doctors can use extraordinary means to keep a patient alive on special machines, but no physician gives written guarantees. In fact, when you are scheduled to have an operation, you are required to sign a release freeing the doctor from responsibility if the operation is not a success. This may serve to deter malpractice suits. You can sue a doctor for poor performance in a medical situation. How can you sue God? He defies the laws of contracts and all legal obligations.

Some mourners turn in rage against the clergyperson. "I am a believer. My mother attended services every week. You saw her. Most of her friends never did. Yet they are alive, and my good, sweet mother is dead. Where is God's justice?" This sort of outburst is made when the "deal" falls through. The family member has prayed and promised to be even more religious. The prayer was not answered. The mourner is sad, frustrated, and angry.

One wise philosopher said that God does answer our prayers, but sometimes the answer is "No." "Yes" answers we joyously accept. The "No" answer tears at the heart. If God, the highest power, fails to act, then where is God's justice? So it is natural to bargain. You may, in desperation, make all sorts of promises. You will treat the dying person with greater respect. You will do splendid acts of charity. You suddenly become very saintlike. You will devote yourself to every worthy cause. Bargaining is born of desperation. It is still another defense mechanism to try to stave off the inevitable demise of a loved one. It is a "running around in circles" to defeat death. The most rational of us can try bargaining. It is the "if only" syndrome. If only You, God, will spare grandfather then I will . . . etc., etc. Promises are easily made. Surely God knows we are sincere, and we are good, too. God will not take away our beloved. God is not cruel. Religion says that God is love. If we could bargain our way into getting God to interfere with nature and curing the patient, it would be truly wonderful. Occasionally we hear of miraculous cures: one who is near death returns to life. The delighted supplicant may say, "My prayers brought Mom back from the edge of death; the prayers worked." As a rabbi, I have often prayed with despairing family members. Sometimes they wish me to pray that their beloved shall have a peaceful end. Most of the time, they are hopeful of recovery. A prayer cannot be a bargain. A prayer expresses a hope. Most religions hold that God responds according to His wishes. His desires and actions are a mystery to us. The person of deep faith can accept death. He or she knows that prayer is not a magic potion to heal the stricken. It should be noted that some religions, for example, Christian Science, hold that through prayer you can be cured; however, Christian Science does not seek to make a deal with God. Bargaining works in human relationships. You cannot bargain for someone's life in exchange for good acts you promise to perform.

Depression

After denial, anger, and bargaining, we may find ourselves in a state of depression. Nothing seems to work. The doctors have given up hope. It is only a matter of days or hours. You wait at the hospital. Hope is gone. Nothing will delay the inevitable. No longer can you deny reality. You are troubled. Your friends cannot cheer you up. Death comes. The depression persists. You complete the funeral arrangements as if in a dream. You are detached from reality. People speak to you, and you go through the motions of saying such things as, "Thank you for stopping over. It is good that you came." The house of mourning is filled with people. They talk, laugh, and may even joke in an effort to cheer you up. You wonder, "How can people talk so normally, when I am being eaten alive by grief?" You may even resent those who are able to smile. You become sensitive. Certain people did not attend the funeral: why not? You are unforgiving. You measure the strength of old friendships by whether or not the friend came to the funeral. Everything is translated into grief.

Depression can be based on real or imaginary concerns. For a child to lose a parent can be a genuine threat. Who will take care of me? If my mother can die, maybe my father will die tomorrow. Unwanted thoughts rush through your mind. Everything is in turmoil and confusion.

If the depression persists, the mourner may seek professional counseling help. Depression is a normal stage for the mourner. The intensity and duration of the mourning are related to the depth of the sense of loss; the greater the attachment to the one who has died, the more intense is the grief.

Some show expressions of grief. This may be because they feel guilty. They did not see their mother very often when she was alive; now everyone has come to see Mom at the funeral, but you cannot talk to her now. Only your own guilt cries out to you.

Severe depression can be triggered by the loss of a loved one. Prolonged grief may be a symptom of other problems. The death may aggravate a condition that now surfaces. Do not be foolish. If you need to talk to your clergyperson, doctor, and good friend, then do so. It is possible to talk one's way out of a depression, depending on the severity of the condition. Doctors can also prescribe antidepressive medicines. There are many ways to treat the severely depressed. The condition should not be allowed to fester. If it is prolonged, action is necessary. Most of us "work out" our grief through talking to friends and becoming active again in the workday or school-day world. Some depression is normal. If it is endless, prompt remedies should be sought. Some suicidal tendencies can grow out of protracted grief. In extreme cases, one might wish to be with one's dead brother or sister. As a teenager, do not be afraid of depression. Do not be afraid to cry. It is good to get it out of your system. People who say, "Don't cry," are wrong. Do not suppress your grief. Express it—let it surface. You will feel better afterward. And if you later suffer moments of depression, this too is common. If you find tears in your eyes at unexpected moments, do not be alarmed. Grief comes out in each of us in different ways. Some cry aloud, others cry inside. Boys have been taught that it is not manly to cry. We know now that this is not correct. Both men and women should be able to show emotion. If you feel like weeping, do so. It may help to relieve your depressed feelings.

Acceptance

After working through depression, Kubler-Ross holds that the final stage is acceptance. When you reach this level, you are able to acknowledge the fact of death. Acceptance means that you can be at ease with yourself. You realize that nothing further can be done. Death has occurred, and no amount of denial, anger, bargaining, or depression will reverse the situation. It may take a considerable amount of time, but once you reach the stage of acceptance, a process of healing begins. You find you can smile. Your appetite returns. Some of your sensitivity wears off. You can laugh, joke, and be with friends. No longer do you suddenly have very "down" feelings. You can talk more easily about the deceased. You may think about him or her every day, but the memories no longer will be so painful. You will recall lovely little moments spent with the person. You may wish to reread some letters and to put the person's picture back on the wall. You can visit places where you once vacationed. Your thoughts will not be totally focused on the deceased. Gradually, you will once again be absorbed into the problems of the world of the living. There is much to do.

The Past Is Gone

In the stage of acceptance, the reality factor takes over. The past cannot be recreated or relived. Gradually it will recede as the problems of the present loom large and immediate.

Those who retreat into the past are really turning their backs on the world. Some people try to keep the dead forever alive. They do not touch his room, leaving everything as it was on the day of the death. Thus, they turn part of their home into a shrine to one who will never return. Morbid dwelling on thoughts of the dead can only be a source of further anxiety and frustration. What is done, is done. Nothing is as truly gone as yesterday.

You may have known persons who simply cannot accept the death of a loved one. This is especially true of happily married couples. The husband dies, and the widow dedicates herself to living the way she thinks he would want her to live. If she interprets this to mean resuming a normal life-style, then a healthy situation ensues. If the widow decides, however, that she can never remarry because no one could "measure up" to her dead husband, you can be certain that trouble is brewing. There is a definite danger in measuring everyone you meet by the standards of the deceased. The dead take on an aura of sanctity. All of their faults are forgotten; only their positive attributes remain. Who can possibly equal them? A golden halo seems to surround them. They may come to seem God-like. This is the beginning of a myth.

Here in America, myths have been developed around Presidents John F. Kennedy and Harry S. Truman. When they were alive, we could see both their strengths and weaknesses. In death, however, sometimes only their strengths are remembered. It is possible, of course—as in the case of Kennedy—that a negative myth can develop to replace the positive one.

If a person is truly loved, the survivors tend to exaggerate the virtues. "My mother did not have an enemy in the world. She never had a harsh word to say about anyone. She was a saint. Everyone loved her." Such comments are frequently made by grieving children. In actual fact, there are few earthly angels. We are human. We become angry and critical. We complain when we are unhappy. We do not like everyone. Some of us are nastier than others. Few have the innate streak of sainthood. Who is perfect? Religion says we are perfectible, but not perfect.

Beyond Acceptance?

Until recently, Kubler-Ross held that acceptance was the final stage of mourning. Now, on the basis of new evidence, she believes that there may be life after death. From interviews with persons who came back from death, she is convinced that if you once see beyond life, you will never fear death.

Doctors tell of reviving persons thought dead and of hearing from them very interesting accounts of the next world. In many cases, the person feels detached from his body. One told of feeling like a detached spirit while watching the doctors work over his body trying to revive him. Most say that a good friend greets you at the moment of death. Some said they were unsure whether they wanted to return to earthly life after experiencing the life-after-death phenomenon. Is there a bright light at the end of the tunnel, beckoning us into the world beyond this life? Freudians would say that a pre-death dream is mere wish-fulfillment. Are these hallucinations or wish-fulfillment moments? No one can say for sure. But the fact that Dr. Kubler-Ross and others take the accounts seriously is enough to give us pause. Those who have had pleasant near-death experiences seem to lose their fear of eventual death. They have seen beyond this life, and what they have witnessed is peaceful, beautiful, and inspiring. Their accounts are in keeping with most Western religious thought, which holds to the idea of a life of the spirit (or soul) after death. What once was greeted with universal skepticism is now seen as a distinct possibility. The doubters are probably in the majority, but the believers in life after death are winning new allies and converts.

Thought Questions

1. Did you ever experience "denial" when you heard of a death?
2. Why are mourners often so angry? Do you share their anger and frustration?
3. Why is it so difficult to bargain with God?
4. How can one move from depression to acceptance when death occurs?
5. Is the past ever really gone?
6. Do you believe that there is life after death, as some now say?

CHAPTER IV

Growing Old

As a young person, you probably seldom think of growing old. When you look at your grandparents, you may say to yourself, "It will be a long time before I look like that." If you live in the suburbs, there may be very few aged persons in your community. I once attended a public-housing hearing to consider a government proposal to build low-cost housing for the aged. One irate citizen got up and shouted, "We don't want a bunch of old faces walking around our town." Among some suburbanites, a strange mentality prevails. They would like to raise their children in an atmosphere where everyone is young, fulfilling a goal of American society.

Today it is a sin to become aged. The cosmetics industry extols the virtues of youth. Magic creams and salves are sold on the promise that they will keep you eternally youthful. Media ads promote all sorts of products to retard the onrushing appearance of age. And when the calendar cannot be denied, cosmetic surgery is used to erase wrinkles and lift sagging chins. Hair coloring is common: "Hate that gray. Comb it away." Men buy hairpieces to achieve a more youthful appearance. The cosmetic surgeon can reshape your nose, as well as almost any other area of your torso.

The highest compliment you can offer your grandmother is to tell her she looks too young to be in that category. To look young and think young is a definite plus.

Our society conspires against the older citizen. Retirement troubles the worker who is active for many years, and suddenly finds himself or herself with too much free time available to fill. Few are ready for retirement, especially the men. America was built on the work ethic. Your job determines your worth. To be a person means to be engaged in some productive activity. The man does not feel himself truly alive if he is idle. Today the woman also competes in the job market. As the modern young woman grows older, she, too, may be singing the "retirement blues." Few men find playing checkers and painting pictures a satisfactory substitute for going to the office. Doctors now speak of the evil of compulsory retirement and its effect on their older patients.

If our society did not place such a premium on youthful vitality and the necessity of a job, the retired male might adjust better to his new condition. It has been suggested that you should begin to prepare for retirement when you are a teenager. Some say that such preparation is a lifelong task. Far too many see the retirement years as useless—a period to mark time until one dies.

The Sociology of Aging

When America was young, most of us lived on farms. Farm life fostered the extended family. As members grew older, rooms could be added to the farmhouse for the elderly. If you were less able to work, your tasks were diminished. No one who was physically fit was retired. On a farm, there was always a job for everyone, from the youngest to the oldest. And when death came, the surviving widow or widower was not alone; a place remained within the extended family.

Today the extended family has been replaced by a smaller unit, called the nuclear family, consisting of parents and one or two children. The industrial age caused people to move from the farm to where jobs were to be found. As farms became mechanized, there was less reason to remain in rural areas. The cities grew. Today few persons live out their lives in one home, in one community. The family goes where the economic opportunities are best. It is probable that you see this pattern of change in your own neighborhood. People come and go. A father is transferred, and your closest friend goes far away. In an age of mobility and change, America is on the go.

Loss of Contact

When people move around so much, the family structure is strained. A young couple starts out in life in the same community as their parents; but, within a few years, either the young family or their parents move to another place. The telephone industry expands rapidly. The phone and the letter become our links with our loved ones. It is easy to lose touch when many miles separate you from your grandparents. If they become too aged or sick to travel, unless you go to visit them (which can be costly), you may seldom if ever see them.

Families face difficult choices. Shall we use Dad's vacation time to travel across the country to visit the grandparents? Or shall we go someplace on our own, where we can have more fun? The very mobility of America tends to separate the generations. Many grandparents languish in retirement villages or health-care facilities, scarcely ever seeing their children or grandchildren. All they have are well-worn little pictures that they carry with them. The sparkle can go out of the eyes if one never sees family and friends. Some give up on life. As one doctor put it, "It seems that some older persons will themselves to die." Life has lost its flavor. Why go on, if no one seems to care?

In life, it is important to be needed and loved. For teenagers, although there may be some periods of rejection, most have a home and parents who care about them. Far too many of the aged live isolated lives, and even when they live in the same town as their children, they are often neglected. Many an oldster will say, "I do not want to make a pest of myself. I do not want to impose on my children and grandchildren." This can become a type of self-rejection.

Too Independent?

If you ask the typical American, he will say he does not wish ever to be a burden on his children. The parent wishes to give. It hurts an aged parent to have to take financial help from his child. American sociology has taught us that independence is a virtue. It is fine to give, but it is terrible to receive. The work ethic says we should be self-supporting. Despair can set in when an older person becomes dependent on his children. Social security benefits do not provide adequate funds to maintain a decent life. Myriad are the articles about older people subsisting in cold-water flats on coffee and rolls —and very little else. When things get desperate enough, an old couple may consider suicide. Death comes in a variety of ways. A feeling of independence can lead to a sense of isolation. "I do not want to be in the way." "I want my children to be happy." "They certainly do not want me around." Tragically, the children may agree. The aged are a bother in the small suburban home or tiny urban apartment. Young people want privacy.

The Scope of the Problem

In 1900, in the United States, there were approximately 3,000,000 persons over the age of 65; one out of every 25 Americans was in that category. Today, we are told that about 22,000,000 Americans are over 65, which is about one out of every 10. In 1900 the life expectancy was about 47 years. Today, you can expect to live to at least age 71 or older. At the same time, the birthrate has been going down. It is now estimated that by the year 2000, some 20 percent of the population will be over 65 or under 15. This means that there will be fewer persons in the work force. Will this reduced number be willing to care for the elderly? Will social security costs be more than the working population can afford to pay? Will the elderly be seen as a burden to an overworked, middle-aged middle class? Is it possible that the elderly will be considered expendable? After all, how much of a strain can any society bear? These could be real questions in the 21st century. Past civilizations, feeling the old to be a burden, led them out into the wilderness to die. Science-fiction books and films envision such future societies in which the old are eliminated. We fear old age today. How much greater would the fear be in an overcrowded world where, unless the old die, there is no room for the young? Science lengthens life. Will longer life make more of us a burden on the strained resources of a shrinking globe? Are resources truly endless? Little preparation is being made for the grim realities of the next century.

The English economist Thomas R. Malthus said that war, disease, and plagues would help maintain the ecological balance of the world. Today, people multiply faster than they die. Wars do not kill on as vast a scale. As science conquers disease, more survive. The "have not" nations may threaten the nations who have great wealth. The elderly could be sacrificed in a future world where there is not enough to go around. In the jungle, the fittest survive. Our planet could conceivably turn into such a place. Hopefully, it will never happen.

Problems of the Aged

One-third of the aged have chronic illnesses. At least 5 percent are homebound. Those who are living at home as invalids are often a great burden to their families. Life can be bleak. It is also estimated that one-third of the elderly live in poverty. Five million of the 22,000,000 live on incomes of less than $2,000 per year. Health care for the poor is usually substandard. It is no wonder that despondent older persons talk so much about suicide. It is one way to get society to notice your plight. Problems tend to multiply as you grow older. Fear of sickness is very real, given the cost of hospitalization today. Even though governmental health plans do offer some financial relief, often the elderly are burdened with filling out numerous forms and going from one government office to the next. It is not unusual for an older person to spend all day criss-crossing town, trying to find the right place to submit the forms. Repayment for money advanced for medical care can be agonizingly slow. Most of the elderly live on fixed incomes, and major illness is a catastrophe.

On the Brighter Side

Not all the elderly are crippled and deserted. There are some who do not live with the constant fear of approaching sickness and death. It has been pointed out that two-thirds of the elderly in America own their own homes in their own communities. Some 70 percent own their own homes, but often they are very humble places. Half a million live in retirement communities. Some are in public or religiously sponsored housing. Those who live in small towns are more likely to occupy their own house. Often they are optimistic about the future. Many are fairly content with their lot in life. Some have managed to save for retirement. All but the most affluent, however, are concerned about the high cost of living.

At times, we see television programs about vigorous oldsters living in the retirement communities of the sun-belt states. Many are tanned, healthy, and active. They have opted for communities that are clean, vital, and usually restricted to a certain age group. Some live on savings, pensions, and social security. Many have been blessed with reasonably good health.

It should also be pointed out that older Americans do have their clubs and lobbying organizations. "Gray power" is now a force to be reckoned with. Politicians do come to speak to the senior citizens —especially during election campaigns.

Thus it should be noted that all is not gloom and doom. You may be lucky enough to have happy grandparents who live a few miles away. Many families are able to make the adjustment to good relations with the grandparents. No two families are alike. There are also situations in which aged parents live happily in the homes of their children. Others live out useful lives in retirement villages or in their own apartments. Governmental agencies are becoming increasingly aware of the problems. As the aged increase in number, their political clout also increases. The old vote in greater numbers than the young and are increasingly vocal in demanding their rights, especially with the threat of cut-backs in their social security benefits.

What Do the Aged Want?

The elderly do not wish to be treated like fossils. I have heard a child say, "Can you imagine my grandmother. At the age of 84, she still drives a car!" Another remark I have heard, "You should see those old people at the Senior Citizen's Center. They are able to dance until the wee hours of the morning." The myth is that if you are old you do not have much energy. Yet in actual fact, a significant number of octogenarians are still active in many fields and professions. Some do enjoy their "golden" years with great vigor and stamina.

Older persons wish to be treated like human beings. Far too often, they are patronized or treated as if they were children. Above all else, if they are in decent health, they wish to be useful and productive. Few of them want to retire. The author Alexander Comfort is quoted as saying, "A good retirement is about two weeks."

Our senior citizens have real needs. They wish to be employed at meaningful labor. Many seek the stimulation of continuing education. The more enlightened colleges are offering a variety of attractive courses for the older students who would like to see the quality of their lives improved and enriched. Many are concerned about receiving adequate medical care if they become ill. They would like to feel that life is not over. Like the rest of us, they want to feel needed.

Whatever your age, you want to be happy. The older person does wish to find meaning and stimulation in his or her life. But grandparents want to be more than baby-sitters. They enjoy being needed in a variety of meaningful roles.

An Interesting Experiment

A number of years ago a friend visiting in the Scandinavian countries saw something that excited her. In one country she found that homes for the aged were built next to orphanages, and the two facilities shared a common recreation area. The elderly had ample free time. The orphans needed foster-grandparents. The older folks were delighted to be of help to the children. The children were flattered that adults actually had time to play with them and listen to them. The aged felt needed, wanted, and loved. The children had the same feeling about these wonderful adults who gave them so much time and attention.

When my friend returned from her trip, she tried to get leaders in her city to implement a similar project, but she soon gave up. She was told it could not be done. Land was expensive. Who would pay the cost of setting up such a facility? She met a myriad of excuses. Her eyes sparkled when she spoke of this wonderful experiment she had seen in Europe. "Why can't we do the same thing here!" she cried. Unfortunately, no one listened to her. It is tragic that good ideas being tried elsewhere are seldom given a hearing in our own country.

When you visit homes for the elderly, there is often an overwhelming sense of depression and mustiness. It is almost as if you were in the very presence of death itself. Yet when a young person comes to visit, the elderly patient perks up. Your being there will make that person's day a truly memorable event.

For those who are idle, time hangs heavy. If you are put away and seldom see family or friends, despair can set in. It then becomes very natural to think about death, even to yearn for it.

The elderly tend to have too much free time. If homes for the elderly could be constructed near orphanages, it would be a boon to both of these rejected segments of society. The old have much wisdom to give to the young. The young can give the old the will to live, knowing that they are needed, wanted, and truly cherished.

I have just spoken of one idea. I am sure many other fresh approaches could be tried. Some communities have programs in which young persons adopt a foster-grandparent. Both profit tremendously. In this world, people do need people. As a young person, never underestimate your importance to your grandparents. Just by being friendly to them, you help them feel that they are not useless and unwanted; and you may be truly lengthening their lives because you care.

A colleague of mine told me of how, when his father was alive, he secretly paid a publisher to hire his father to review books. His father enjoyed reading. He never knew that his son was really providing the salary he received for writing book reviews. I am sure that this son's act of kindness did much to prolong his father's life.

There was a play on Broadway, *Tuscaloosa's Calling Me . . . But I'm Not Going,* by Hank Beebe and Hill Heyer, in which the main character sang a song called "Backwards." The lyrics said, in effect, "would not it be wonderful if we were born old, and gradually grew younger?" Ultimately, we would return to our mother's womb, rather than be buried in the cemetery. Each year we would have fewer wrinkles and gray hairs. Each succeeding stage of life would be more livable, because we would have the wisdom of the older stage to draw on. When we moved from old age to middle age, we would not be intolerant of our wives and children. We would know, with biblical wisdom, that "this too shall pass." Young adulthood would not terrify us, since we had already been beyond that stage. Adolescence would be more bearable, since we would have already lived our future life. In the song, the actor says—in effect—that God made a mistake. If only He had reversed things and we could begin in old age and grow backward, it would be a happier world! Of course, this is a fantasy.

The aged have the years of experience, but many lack the energy to use their talents. Our society should examine its values. In an earlier age, the elder was respected. In some Eastern societies, when you walk past an older person, you must physically lower yourself, so as not to be taller than he is. It is true that just living a long time is no guarantee of wisdom. Age in itself can bring wisdom or foolishness. It depends upon the individual.

The Aged as a Special Treasure

Our older persons are very special. In a class I taught, I asked the children to interview their grandparents and bring back either written or taped reports. The children learned a great deal, and the oldsters were flattered that the children cared enough to record what they had to say. I asked each student to create a chronology and to work up a family tree of his or her family. In this way, the child could seek his roots in his past. Other projects may suggest themselves. When you feel wanted, you do not brood about dying. When you are busy living, you do not think about death. Your acts of kindness and concern for the elderly can give them added vital years of life. All of us, if we are fortunate, will live to a ripe, vigorous advanced stage of awareness. Yes, the older person is a special treasure. Respect begets respect. The measure of the worth of a civilization may well be how it treats the elderly. A civilization that has no compassion for its older members is not truly worthy. It was a Jewish sage who wrote, "Gauge a country's prosperity by its treatment of the aged."

A Story

It is recorded in an ancient legend, that in a far-off place there dwelt a family. The grandfather had a lovely room in a place of honor. As the family increased in size, the grandfather gradually was given less. He was moved, finally, to the barn and lived in a very humble manner. One day the father of the house saw his young son playing in the attic. The boy was arranging some rags in a heap. "What are you doing?" the father asked. "Oh," said the son, "these rags are for you." "Why for me?" asked the father. The son replied, "I have seen how you take care of grandfather, so I am preparing these ragged garments for you, dear father, when you are old and I will be taking care of you." The child learns by the model he sees in the home. The sociology of the American home offers little or no room for many of the elderly. One wonders whether this trend will continue for the future?

An unknown author wrote the following poem called "Who Will Take Grandma?" It expresses a problem in America today:

> Who will take Grandma, who will it be?
> All of us want her, I'm sure you will agree.
> Let's call a meeting—let's gather the clan,

GROWING OLD

In such a big family, there's certainly one
Willing to give her a place in the sun.

Strange how we thought she'd never wear out,
But see how she walks; it's arthritis no doubt!
Kissed away troubles, and mended our dreams
Wonderful Grandma, we all loved her so
Isn't it dreadful, she has nowhere to go.

One little corner is all she would need.
A shoulder to cry on, her Bible to read,
A chair by the window with sun coming through,
Some pretty spring flowers, still covered with dew.

Who will warm her with love so she won't mind the cold,
Oh, who will take Grandma now that she's old?
What! Nobody wants her? Oh yes, there is one
Willing to give her a place in the sun,

Where she won't have to worry, or wonder or doubt,
And she won't be our problem to worry about.
Pretty soon now, God will give her a bed,
But who'll dry our tears when dear Grandma is dead?

Thought Questions

1. Have you ever thought about growing old? Does it frighten you?
2. Why do you think adults are afraid of aging?
3. Someday, would you want to bring your parents into your home if they were ill and aged?
4. What do you think the aged really want?
5. Do you enjoy visiting your grandparents?
6. How do grandparents (or other aged persons) react to seeing you?
7. Is there a way for youth to spend more time with the elderly? Would this be advisable?
8. How do you react to the poem at the end of this chapter?

CHAPTER V

The Living Will

One of the new developments in recent years is called the "living will." Even as it is possible to will parts of your body to medical science so as to prolong life, it is also possible to arrange in advance the manner of your death.

The living will is an attempt to prevent extraordinary means from being used to keep you alive. The concept has been recognized by law in California, North Carolina, Oregon, Texas, New Mexico, Vermont, Washington, Idaho, Kansas, Nevada, Alabama and Arkansas.

The purpose of the living will is to allow you to exert control over how you will be medically treated, should you be dying of an incurable illness. A model has been drawn up by the Concern For Dying, 250 West 57th Street, New York, N.Y. 10019. A copy may be had on request. The document reads as follows:

Death is as much a reality as birth, growth, maturity, and old age. It is the one certainty of life. If the time comes when I,_____ _____, can no longer take part in decisions for my own future, let this statement stand as an expression of my wishes, while I am still of sound mind. If the situation should arise in which there is no reasonable expectation of my recovery from physical or mental disability, I request that I be allowed to die and not be kept alive by artificial means or heroic measures. I do, however, ask that medication be mercifully administered to me to alleviate suffering even though this may shorten my remaining life. This statement is made after careful consideration and is in accordance with my strong convictions and beliefs. I want the wishes and directions here expressed carried out to the extent permitted by law. Insofar as they are not legally enforceable, I hope that those to whom this Will is addressed will regard themselves as morally bound by these provisions.

Signed _____

Date _____

Witness _____

Witness _____

Copies of this request have been given to _____

_____

_____

_____

The above living will has been widely distributed. Persons are signing them and witnessing them in the hope that their requests will be honored should the occasion arise. In an age when science prolongs life, more and more of us are subject to terminal illnesses that can be terribly painful. The living will seeks to ease our way into the next world with as little delay as possible and with a swift and merciful ending to our suffering. Let us analyze the living will.

Death Is as Much a Reality as Birth

The will recognizes that death is real. Our society minimizes this. Death is cosmetically concealed. People do not die, they "pass on." Our dead are "in repose" in a casket. Often they look very lifelike. The word death is hard to accept; it is so very final. Even though Western religions teach that birth and death are part of the life process, the thought of thanatos—the death instinct—is repugnant. Perhaps you have heard friends say, "I dread going to a funeral. It makes me feel terrible. Why do we have to talk about death?" It is a painful subject. Our own deaths are far off. We cannot picture how the world would be without us. Will we go to sleep when we die? Will we awaken and see a great light? Is there a heaven and a hell? Everyone thinks about such things, but to dwell on them is morbid. The living will is merely being realistic. Yes, people do die. It can happen to anyone, at whatever age. The will is an attempt to be logical and pragmatic about a fact of the human experience. All human beings on this earth will eventually die. A new generation will be born. So, "Death is as much a reality as birth, growth, maturity, and old age. It is the one certainty of life."

I Make This Statement While Still of Sound Mind

The living will seeks to exert control while you still have the power of choice. Once you are stricken and confined to a hospital bed, matters of choice are largely taken out of your hands. The hospital staff attends to your needs. Family and friends come and go. You may even overhear conversations as relatives try to decide what to do about you. You may also detect attitudes of the doctors concerning your chances of getting well. Often the doctors enter into a conspiracy with the family to conceal the truth. You may never be told that you are dying. You may go to your death without ever knowing that you are terminally ill.

So, if you have strong feelings, now is the time to get them down in writing, properly witnessed, and filed with your survivors as well as with your legal representatives. It is always better to make decisions when you are healthy and can think without the burden of pain. The comatose patient is beyond controlling his destiny. By making plans in advance, you relieve your family of the most difficult decision they may ever have to make—whether to keep you alive (knowing that your case is hopeless) or to let you die with dignity and speed. What good are a few extra days, weeks, or months if you exist only by virtue of machines?

What you have to decide is whether you wish to make the decision or leave it to others. It is not easy. There may be the fear that treatment will be stopped too soon. We all have read of cases where persons in a coma come out of it after many months of being given up for lost. It is not a decision to be made or taken lightly.

I Request That I Be Allowed to Die

You cannot demand compliance. The law is still vague, except in California; and even there, the will might still be questioned. Your relatives may even act against your wishes, feeling that the sick really do not know what is good for them. It is not enough to file away the will. It is vital that you talk over its provisions with your family and get their promise to fulfill what you want done. Often, even with a will, the family falters. They love you. They are loath to give up hope. How could they forgive themselves if you died, and a week later the cure for cancer were found? So the most we can do is to make the request, being fully aware that our own desires can be thwarted. I have known of instances in which burial instructions prepared prior to death have not been followed. Persons who request cremation may ultimately receive a conventional funeral. A simple handwritten note to the family, kept in the safe, is not sufficient. The living will is fully attested to and witnessed. A formal document carries greater weight. It may be of sufficient force to allow you to die with dignity.

We know how difficult it is to achieve a request for a speedy death. Even those who are living on Death Row and request death may find their wishes thwarted. Such was the case in 1977 in Utah of a convicted murderer, Gary Mark Gilmore. Even though the Utah Supreme Court by a vote of 41 to 1 ruled that he had the right to die "like a man" before a firing squad, the Governor referred the matter to the Pardon Board. Whatever the outcome of cases such as Gilmore's, it is clear that even murderers have little control over the right to die. Gilmore demanded quick death at age 35 rather than to spend the rest of his life in prison. Obviously, to him, a life sentence was a type of slow death. Ultimately, his wish to be executed was granted.

Joseph E. Davis, on Death Row in New York, was quoted as saying, "Death Row is the roughest experience a man could have to face. You are cut off from the rest of the world and from the rest of the prison, and you seldom see anybody other than the guard who is always outside your cell. You never know if this will be the day when they come for you and say, 'This is it.' This place could burn down and I would be the last to know it." [1]

The prisoner experiences mental torture. He may long for death. Yet, ironically, society is reluctant to grant his wish. In like manner, the hospitalized patient, suffering each day, also finds that he lacks control over life and death. Although a woman can control whether or not to abort a pregnancy (according to law), the person who is terminally ill has little control over his treatment.

---

[1] New York *Times*, Nov. 14, 1976.

No Artificial Means or Heroic Measures

If you have been in hospitals and have seen anguished families standing long hours beside comotose, terminally ill persons who are hooked up to machines, you are aware of the cruelty of the situation. In effect, the terminally ill are controlling the healthy ones. The family feels compelled to be in attendance. They are being drained physically and emotionally—and also financially. The cost in dollars can be staggering. No one begrudges money when there is hope of recovery, but one questions the wisdom of endlessly prolonging the life of those reduced to being little more than a vegetable.

If you truly love the dying patient, are you doing him or her a favor? Might not ultimate peace be a better answer? This is the kind of decision that must come from you. There are recorded cases of mothers who literally sat for years at the bedside of hopelessly ill children who never regained consciousness. What can one say of such self-sacrifice? Is this the best role for the grieving mother? Is the "hope" of cure and that the doctors are wrong a sufficient basis for a year-long vigil? The maternal instinct to protect the young can be overpowering. Who is to say what are the moral dimensions of how we act?

I Do Not Fear Death

The will says that the writer is not as fearful of death as of ". . . the indignities of deterioration, dependence, and hopeless pain." Torturers know that one way to reduce the will to resist is by destroying the victim's sense of dignity and worth. This can be done by both physical and mental torture. We have all read about brainwashing. Not everyone can resist the authority that browbeats us into submission. The living will seeks to validate your right not to waste away. It tries to avoid the crippling effects of looking in the mirror and truly seeing your own death. I have gone into hospital rooms that have the smell of death. The person may be physically present but spiritually and emotionally be but a shell of the former self. Should such a life be prolonged? Might it not be more humane to let the patient die with a degree of self-honor and awareness?

It is terrible to watch a loved one deteriorate, day by day. It hurts to see a once vigorous and robust person reduced to dependence and helpless, agonizing pain. One can look in their eyes and almost see a cry for help. It is no wonder that the terminally ill have begged for death. In one case on Long Island, a young man acceded to his brother's request and shot him, to put him out of his pain. The act was against the law, but the courts did show mercy in his case. Society understands the anguish. We can sympathize with those who are being begged by a loved one to be spared further days of agony. Yet, the courts do not condone active euthanasia. The doctor who gives a patient an overdose of a drug to put that person out of pain may wind up in jail. Our life does not belong to us. Society has the major say in what becomes of you and me.

Medication to Hasten Death

If medicines act to speed death, this might be considered "active" euthanasia. The popular definition, however, is that if one gradually withdraws treatment while giving enough pain-killers to permit the patient to die peacefully, this is not murder. Society is not yet ready to accept active euthanasia, but passive euthanasia is gaining favor.

The living will seeks the administering of whatever useful means are available to bring about death with a minimum of pain and discomfort. One can see why doctors may hesitate. Suppose the survivors change their minds? What if they later say, "Doctor, you knew better. Why did you let us talk you into doing this?" Physicians are all too aware of malpractice cases. Suit could be brought, and it could be claimed that the family was in an agitated state, unable to think clearly. The living will does give some legal support to the action of the doctor, making him less vulnerable. The document does have moral weight. In time, it may have full legal weight as well.

By temperament and training, a doctor's major function is to prolong life. The question is, what is life? Is life defined in terms of a heartbeat when the brain is gone? Human life seems to demand more than breathing. Awareness and feeling and expression are components of the human life processes. If only the heart is left, what good is it to be merely alive? Slowly and reluctantly, the medical profession is coming to the conclusion that "death with dignity" must be a very real option. If there were no fear of legal recourse, I am certain that many more acts of euthanasia would take place. One doctor pointed out that in a county hospital with only a certain number of respirators, who is to decide who is to have the machines, and who is to die? Decisions of life and death can be forced on society. Suppose there are a limited number of kidney machines and a multitude of patients? Who shall have the machines? Who shall be left to die? So, in a way, euthanasia-type decisions are being made daily where limited facilities exist to sustain life for patients who are not terminally ill but do require a machine to survive.

Be Morally Bound by This Mandate

The living will still has little legal sanction in most states. It is more of a moral than a legal document. The living will is a cry for compliance. It urges your relatives to respect your wishes, not *their* wishes. It seeks to persuade them that you are truly serious in your hope that a dignified death will not be denied to you. It tries to overcome the normal questions in the minds of your survivors: Am I really doing the best thing? Suppose by a miracle the illness recedes? The living will does not have as its goal the wish to have the doctor play the role of God. All it tries to accomplish is the peaceful end to a human life.

What is more merciful? Shall we prolong life by artificial means, hoping against hope that the patient will "snap out of it," sit up in bed, and say I'm fine? Or should we authorize the authorities to act with dispatch when a patient is truly terminal and beyond any reasonable hope of returning to a normal existence. There is no doubt but that a small percentage of those who are allowed to die might have miraculously regained health. We will never know. The nagging doubt of taking a life unnecessarily will always be present. Where there is life, there is some hope. Yet if the statistical hope is one in several million, what choice do we have? I am not recommending that persons be forced to sign a living will. It seems to me, however, that the rights of the terminally suffering patient should be respected. The living will makes it easier for the family. They can respect the patient's wishes if they are not swayed by the emotions of guilt and fear. Many persons shy away from making tough choices. Decision-making is a casualty of the 20th century. Death is a "turn-off" for most persons. In America, our goal is happiness, not pain.

THE LIVING WILL

Decisions about death are painful. We would rather not be the one to decide when euthanasia is under consideration.

Think About It

Put yourself in the patient's place. He is living with agony. All hope is gone. He goes from a comotose state to a brief state of consciousness. He sees the grief on your faces. You may not have even told him how sick he is. The patient is confused. He senses that he is not getting better. He has read enough and seen enough on television to know that he may have an incurable disease. Yet his intelligence is insulted. He is not told the truth because the family fears that the truth will destroy his will to live. Artificial conversations take place. The patient is dying. He senses it. You know it. The doctor consults with you: shall special respirators and unusual means be used to prolong life? You have to make the decision. If a living will exists, you can give the answer after consulting with others in the family. If there is no living will, more of the burden is upon the relatives. The doctor has a vital role to play. He can tell you the odds for survival and in what condition the patient will be if placed on life-sustaining machines. But as society is structured, the doctor cannot make the final decision. That last word is in the survivor's hands. If the patient is lying in a bed of continual pain, his answer—I am sure—is obvious. The end of pain is paramount. All that the living will hopes to do is to let him die with a degree of dignity, and not be kept alive endlessly and for no useful purpose.

Preamble to the Living Will

The preamble says, "To my family, my physician, my lawyer, my clergyman—to any medical facility in whose care I happen to be—to any individual who may become responsible for my health, welfare, or affairs." This is an effort to spread the responsibility for the execution of the will to a wide variety of persons. The decision becomes a shared one. The signer of the will is confident that this wide variety of people will ultimately come to respect the wishes expressed in the will. I feel that the preamble is very necessary. By demanding input from doctors, family, lawyers, and clergy, it sets the stage for death with dignity, which is its goal.

I found it of interest that, among others, the clergy are to be consulted. Some religions would be against the provisions of the living will. If your life is in God's hands, then only God can take your life. It is possible that a few clergypersons would feel that all means must be used to sustain life. One religious tradition says, "He who saves one life, is as if he has saved the entire world." But what kind of life have you saved? When is life really life? Theologians may argue about such matters. Philosophers may talk of the meaning of existence. A pragmatic situation exists. A patient is dying. He or she has given you a living will clearly stating what is to be done in such a circumstance. Can you, in good conscience, defy the patient's wishes? This is something that more and more of us will have to consider, as living wills become increasingly popular and available. If they ultimately are given legal approval, the patient's family may have less about which to feel guilty.

Why So Few Living Wills?

There can be a real fear on the part of some that the living will could be used to hasten the death of an elderly rich person. Suppose there are greedy relatives, eager to see an old uncle or aunt quickly in the grave. If you are elderly and do not trust your family, you might think long and hard about the wisdom of signing such a document. Then, too, if you do not trust the medical profession, you might hesitate. Doctors are often wrong. No two doctors seem to agree about anything. Consultants called in on a difficult case do not invariably reach a consensus. Misdiagnosis is more common than we realize. Everyone has heard horror stories of what occurs in some hospitals. In the papers we read of unscrupulous doctors who are totally unskilled, and of unnecessary surgery. Theories about illnesses and how to cure them change from one day to the next. There has been a loss of faith in the absolute wisdom of the medical profession. We go to doctors when we are ill, but we question them more closely than we did a generation ago. So many drugs have proven to be harmful.

It is true that the more we know the less we really know. The human body is a wondrous and diverse vessel. It often acts contrary to the laws of statistics. The human being is unpredictable. The physicians are not the gods of our century. We turn to them for help, yet not everyone looks upon them as the last word. This only adds to the difficulty inherent in writing a living will. In order to write it, you must believe that your doctors know what they are doing and that there is more than a reasonable chance that they are right. Before writing such a will, you will probably discuss it with family, friends, and others. You might wish to show the will to your family doctor and get his opinion. It would also be wise to consult an attorney to determine how much legal weight it will have. Above all else, you should be very sure in your own mind that this is what you really want to do. Then, if you make the decision, it is based on research and thought. It should be noted, however, that you can cancel the living will if in the future you decide it is unwise.

Another Option

Ours is a world of multiple choices. The living will is another choice to make. If you are young, the will may seem foolish. But, suppose you are in a serious automobile accident and are lingering between life and death? Suppose you sustain terrible injuries that rob you of the power to think? Would you want to be attached to a machine for an indefinite period? Would you cause your family more—or less—grief if you had a living will? If you are under the age of 18, the will would have little legal force. It would be a purely moral document, a statement of your wishes, as expressed to your parents. In any event, this is an area of limited choice, since the living will has legal support in only one state. The most it can do is point a direction. It does indicate that you have confidence that your family, together with the doctors, clergypersons, and lawyers, can be helpful in deciding your fate. If it does nothing more than this, it might be a source of comfort to those who, having given the matter serious thought, do reach the decision to sign the living will.

California Acts

It should be noted that in August, 1976, California became the first state in the nation to enact "death with dignity" legislation. Governor Edmund G. Brown, Jr., signed the Natural Death Act on September 30, 1976. An editorial in the Los Angeles *Times* of Sept. 8 said, "The bill, amended many times since its introduction last February, is not without faults. But the principle it embodies is a humane and necessary one." The California law provides that adults have the right to control the medical care given to them. The patient in California now has the right to reject treatment that interferes with the process of dying. This is a monumental step. The California law allows you to exercise your rights through a written, witnessed declaration that can be revoked at any time. California has pioneered in this new approach to control of one's life. It remains to be seen how many other states will follow suit. And one wonders if the California law will be tested in the Supreme Court of the United States as to whether it is constitutional. For the moment, it seems, the law is valid in one state. Students of euthanasia will be studying the effects of the law in the years ahead.

Thought Questions

1. Would you consider having a living will for yourself?
2. What are the advantages of the living will?
3. What are the disadvantages of the living will?
4. Do you think that more states will legalize the living will, as time goes by?
5. Why might some persons be afraid to sign a living will?
6. Do you feel the opinions of doctors can be trusted?

CHAPTER VI

The Cost of Dying

It is often difficult for people to understand the large costs involved in a funeral. Such persons forget that there is also a significant cost involved when we come into this world. Maternity care is not cheap. Hospital costs have skyrocketed in the past few years. The average cost of a semiprivate room has risen to over $350 per day in many metropolitan areas. Fees charged by hospitals, doctors, and other health specialists keep increasing. The same is true in the funeral industry. Today gravediggers are organized and at times have gone on strike. Salaries for those in the funeral profession have risen. No industry (and the funeral industry is just that—an industry) is exempt from galloping inflation. It has been pointed out that there are four separate and distinct categories of charges that make up the cost of a funeral. In a brochure published by the National Funeral Directors Association, the costs are listed as follows:

1. Those that specifically involve the funeral director, including his professional services and those of his staff; the use of his facilities and equipment; and the casket and the vault selected.
2. Those dealing with the disposition of the body. If earth-interred, there is the cost of the grave (if no cemetery lot is previously owned) and the charge for opening and closing it. If cremated, there is the charge for actual cremation, plus the cost of an urn for the remains if one is desired.
3. Those for memorialization, such as a monument or marker for the grave or a niche for the urn of cremated remains.
4. Those miscellaneous expenses paid by the family directly or through the funeral director. These include such items as flowers, newspaper death notices, additional limousines, burial clothing, and out-of-town transportation of the body.

In a 1971 survey by the National Funeral Directors Association, it was pointed out that Americans paid $983 for the "average" regular adult funeral they selected. In a newspaper article [1] the reporter stated that an average cost of death is $2,500. This figure included the cost of the cemetery plot, marker, and vault, as well as the funeral itself. "Some of the services provided by undertakers are: embalming the body, arranging floral displays, posting obituary notices in the newspaper, and transporting the coffin to the cemetery." The National Funeral Directors might disagree with this estimate. In New York State, funeral directors are required to itemize their costs; "package" funerals are against the law in New York.

Free Funerals?

You may wonder why it should cost money to die. When you think about it, however, everything in life (and apparently in death as well) has a price. It is possible to find low-cost burial associations or societies in some parts of the country. There are religious groups that band together and form nonprofit burial societies, which make possible lower burial costs. But there does seem to be a psychological need to follow current custom. This means that, for most middle-class families, the four items of cost (listed earlier) become mandatory. It has been argued that when a family member dies, you do not have time to "shop around" to see where you can get the best price on a casket. When you select a funeral director, he normally carries through for the entire procedure. Criticism has been leveled at the display of caskets in the showroom. Some funeral directors have been criticized for "pushing" more expensive caskets. In my own experience as a clergyman, I have found a minimum of criticism in this area. Most people tell me that when they go to select a casket, they are free to look at all of them, in each price range. What must be understood is that people often have a certain image in their minds. If the person who has died has been upper-middle-class all his life, the survivors may feel that the moment of death should be dignified by an appropriately expensive casket. Some religions—among them Judaism—deem a plain wooden casket to be

---

[1]New York *Times*, Sept. 26, 1981.

sufficient. A majority, however, usually prefer to follow the current custom, which says—in effect—that the day of death should reflect the style of the person's life. It has even been pointed out that some ethnic groups favor very expensive funerals, far beyond the lifestyle of the deceased. Some families will finance funeral costs over a period of years in order to provide a truly worthy burial. Critics of the funeral industry hold that the industry caters too much to these "class" and "status" feelings. Others hold that the industry is basically giving the consumer what he or she wants. They will say, "We could not stay in business if we did not maintain modern, up-to-date parlors, the latest equipment in limousines, facilities, and the like." The public has a certain image. The funeral industry works within the current sociological attitudes and postures of the public. In my own experience, I have found most funeral directors to be sympathetic and helpful to the mourners.

Problems for the Industry

There is some indication that regulation of the funeral industry is in sight. The Federal Trade Commission has been running a three-year investigation of it. Any $2 billion dollar a year industry is bound to be investigated. State licensing boards now regulate the nation's 22,000 funeral homes. Most, it should be pointed out, are small local enterprises. The F.T.C. seeks to crack down on some questionable practices. It is investigating how caskets are displayed, why coffins have to be burned during cremation, and the advisability of "package" one-cost funerals. The F.T.C., in effect, would like to encourage families to be able to comparison-shop for the cost of funerals. This, they feel, might bring the prices down. A declining death rate in 1982 has been viewed with calmness by the industry. The spokesmen for the industry feel that theirs is a true service industry. Someone must be on the premises of a funeral home 24 hours a day. It is an emergency business in which quick action is required. Death does not announce itself. The morticians can be busy one day and then have long intervals of inactivity.

One new trend to meet rising costs is to establish a chain of funeral homes. Equipment can thus be shared. A hearse that cost $13,000 in the late 1960's can now require an outlay of $25,000.

The average person does not think in such terms. When death occurs, we want prompt help at reasonable cost.

As with every industry, the people in the funeral profession have their critics. Doctors are under fire for shady practices. The public looks askance at lawyers. No profession stands pure and blameless. The funeral industry stresses the comfort it gives to survivors rather than the cost of dying. I have heard people say, "It was truly amazing. My father died in Florida. The funeral director took care of all the arrangements to get the body shipped back by plane to New York. It was done quickly and efficiently." Funeral directors do have contacts all over the country. They are usually efficient and helpful to the survivors. From my own observations, they are helpful also in cushioning the shock that death brings to a family. In truth, they are working with people at a time when nerves are frayed and anger is often close to the surface. Tempers are often short. They have a delicate task to perform, as the survivors begin to cope with their grief, guilt, fears, and frustrations.

Viewing—Good or Bad?

Viewing of the body is a widespread practice in America, but it is not new. Many ancient cultures have done this. Critics of the funeral industry say that the practice is designed to get the public into their parlor and to think about using their services if they should have such a need. Those more kindly disposed to the industry say that this is just another service offered to the mourners. Sometimes the mourners do not wish to have company in their home the day before the funeral. Going to the funeral parlor allows them to greet many friends who may not be able to go to the actual funeral service. Also, if people come to your home, it must be spotless, and hospitality demands that you offer food and drink.

Viewing the body removes these pressures. The casket can be open or closed. Some religions, among them Judaism, frown upon the open casket. But even here, the Jewish clergy are not all of one mind. Most hold that it is better to remember the individual in life, rather than to have as a final image the dead body. Others, among them some physicians, hold that it is healthy to view the dead. In this way one faces up to the reality of death and is less likely later to have thoughts that the dead are still alive or have just "gone away" and will soon return.

There is no consensus about viewing. It has its champions and its detractors. A clergyperson will be glad to discuss the matter with the survivors if approached about it. In some communities it is the custom to view the body, and if you feel bound by custom you probably will do it. Some have a strong desire for a last look at the deceased. Others would prefer to remember them in life. The survivors are free to tell the funeral director whether or not they wish to have viewing.

The Psychological Cost

In my experience, few complaints are voiced about the economic cost of funerals. It is true that some feel the charges are unfair. However, when the bill is itemized (as is done by law in New York), the survivors can be somewhat selective in keeping costs down. I have noticed that fewer limousines are used when funeral costs are itemized. Beyond the problem of cost are the emotional factors wrought by the death itself. This psychological cost is seen in a number of different ways and can be long-lasting.

Guilt

After almost every death, the survivors have a sense of guilt. Sometimes they overcompensate for this by holding an elaborate and expensive funeral. What they failed to give a loved one in life, they will grant in death. There is also genuine guilt. Some children have mistreated their parents. Others who have put a parent in a home for the aged are overcome with grief and guilt when the parent dies shortly after entering such a facility. "I saw my mother fading in the nursing home, but I lacked the strength to bring her into my own house." These and similar sentiments are echoed by the survivors. So, if one feels guilty, he will continue for a long time—possibly forever—to have such feelings.

"Why did I not help my brother when he needed me?" Yes, some have the Messiah complex: if a person dies it is his fault; he should have been the heavenly rescuer of the stricken. Or someone will say,

"If only I had taken Dad to a different doctor . . ." The list is endless, even as the guilt feelings go on and on. The cost of guilt cannot be measured in money. Many would gladly pay a large amount of cash to be rid of guilt. When the problem is extreme, visits to a psychologist can be helpful.

Feelings of guilt sometimes return when the survivors enter a house of worship. In the presence of the minister, they may relive their real or imagined sins. I have known persons who simply cannot come to pray because of this. To be in church or synagogue makes them aware of their own failings. Or, in a mood of both guilt and anger, they may blame God for taking a loved one from them.

It would be nice if the guilt-ridden could go before a civil court and plead their case to a judge; hearing him rap with the gavel and say, "Not guilty," would remove the heaviness from the heart. However, such tribunals do not exist, so the guilty go on judging and blaming themselves. They sentence themselves to long, cruel punishment, with the wish "If only I had done differently." If one is truly guilty of offenses against the dead, then the superego can inflict constant punishment. Even more tragic are those who feel guilty when they are innocent. No one is all-powerful. No one can be with a person 24 hours a day. I have seen persons drive themselves to an early death over fancied and imagined guilt. With such persons, there are usually other difficult psychological components, such as loss of an authority figure. Excessive thoughts of grief can lead to severe depression. When guilt persists, it should not be treated lightly. It can be the forerunner of severe problems for the survivors.

Facing Death

Death has now become a fact of life. It would seem that much more appears about it in the media. The magazine *Psychology Today* noted that when it ran a questionnaire on death, more than 30,000 readers replied; this was 10,000 more than had replied to a questionnaire on sex.

There has been a change in the place of death. In an earlier age, people died in their homes and were buried from their homes. When America was a frontier country, the funeral director did not play the role he plays today. Times have changed. People are more likely to die in a hospital and be buried from a funeral home. So when it comes to facing death, there are special problems. Our minds must be attuned to visiting the dying one in a hospital. Although many would prefer to die at home, few homes are equipped to cope with the severely ill patient. Medical health insurance also tends to make it more feasible financially to die in the hospital. Who can afford private nurses and doctors in one's home? Some brave persons do keep dying family members with them at home; yet the strain on the family is tremendous. When all the attention is directed toward the dying member, the others may feel neglected and forsaken. How much of our time and energy is owed to the dying? What sort of priority must be given to the living?

Suppose your grandfather is critically ill. Your parents decide to bring him into their home. He suffers from a lingering illness and needs constant attention. At night, he cries out for his pain-killing pill. Your parents are distraught. They fear they are neglecting you, their child, because Grandfather requires such close care. You may even hear them cry out in anguish, "Why doesn't God take Grandfather? Why must he go on suffering?" But to voice such a thought creates feelings of guilt and frustration. Your parents feel helpless. The finest doctors cannot bring Grandfather back to health. He is reduced to skeleton proportions. He may even say, "Why don't I die? I am such a burden to the family." Most families at this point will—if they can—put the dying patient into some sort of terminal-care facility. It is not that they do not love the person. They may well be physically, mentally, and emotionally exhausted from caring for him. It is no wonder that most prefer to face their own death (as well as the death of a loved one) in a hospital. We are not as stoic as our ancestors. Also, they did not have the life-prolonging medicines and machines that we use on a routine basis.

A Developmental Process

As discussed earlier in this book, Dr. Kubler-Ross was able to define the stages of dying. Now we hear more and more about looking upon death as the culmination of the various stages of life. Yet, with all our sophistication it is not easy to face. One study pointed out that physicians are even more afraid of death than most other people. They may even fear death more than those who are terminally ill. Of course, I imagine other studies could be made to show contrary opinions. But the fact that doctors themselves are not really prepared to face death (even though they work with and fight it daily) is something of a shock to hear. We usually picture the doctor as a brave man who devotes his life to the healing arts. Such a gallant warrior surely cannot be afraid of death, his ultimate foe.

Sad to say, the physician is as susceptible as you or I to the fear of death. Some now see death as a "process." At each step of the way, a person needs help to cope with the ultimate reality. Some hospitals now have "dying counselors," who are available to be with the patient and the family as the final hours draw near. So far, this is not a formalized profession. Dying counselors can include doctors, clergy, nurses, social workers, and others. Some are beginning to make dying counseling a full-time occupation. They work with the patients and their families, trying to help them to express openly their fear, anger, and frustration. Often, the survivors need to get their lives in order. Someone, for example, may have to talk to the dying patient about revising his will and having his attorney bring certain vital papers to the hospital room. There are practical as well as psychological needs to be met. It is quite possible that dying counseling may become a full-time profession demanding special skills of empathy and knowledge of human nature.

We note that courses and seminars on death and dying are becoming part of the training of the professionals in the health fields. As doctors, nurses, clergy, and others become more conversant with the techniques to be used, the process of death can be better faced by the dying and the family. Increasingly, more books on the theme of death are being published. In less than ten years, one bibliography on death grew from 400 to over 2,600 items. Publishers do not put out books on a subject unless there is public interest in it. In fact, one research study revealed that students in the 1980's are more preoccupied with thoughts of death than were students surveyed in the 1930's. This implies that today's generation of students think about death often. One new researcher says that most teenagers at some time or another have thought about suicide. Death is not far from the human mind. When I ask little children what they pray for, one of the frequent answers is that there should be no more war and death—or they will say, "I wish my grandma was alive." This hunger for eternal life starts at an early age. Death is seen as an affront to everything we are or hope to be. That last trip to the funeral home, where the deceased is laid out in a casket, is very emotion-charged and gives pause for thought even to those who have strong faith in the immortality of the soul.

A Healthy Development?

A French social historian, Philippe Aries, has argued that the fascination with death is a healthy human development. Such concerns foreshadowed the collapse of the Middle Ages, but also pointed to the new flowering of the love of life that was to follow. It may be that if we are aware of death as a process, we will come to fear it a bit less; but this is not at all certain today. Ernest Beck in his book *The Denial of Death* puts forth the argument that a person becomes a hero because he is terrified by death. So one might argue that the hero is the one who goes forth to battle and returns. To face death is to rehearse a great victory, according to Beck. Few of us seek such heroic moments. Philosophically, the notion may have validity. In everyday life, death is something to be avoided. This may be why we go to such pains to disguise death. Before we place all the blame on the funeral industry, we must ask ourselves whether they are not catering to our own needs to beautify death and remove the ugliness of its reality.

Each person needs his or her own way to cope with facing the death of a loved one. There is no one pat solution. Some have a psychological need for a large, expensive funeral; others opt for a simple and less expensive burial. Some need large monuments. For others, a simple marker is sufficient. Some favor in-ground burial. Others say, "My beloved must go into a mausoleum." It is a case of "to each his own." So long as options are available, we are, I feel, on safe ground. Critics will always be among us. Choice is important. Investigations of funeral practices are inevitable. No industry of such magnitude and far-reaching effect can be without some abuses. Every major industry is bound to be watched by the government, and the funeral field is no exception. Costs will rise so long as inflation continues; and some will band together to form associations to bring down the cost, even as persons form "cooperatives" to avoid the high costs at the supermarket.

For you, it may be difficult to think of the funeral industry as a business. I have heard people say, "Ugh, the business of death. It is awful." The more thoughtful realize that help is needed when a beloved one dies. To the extent that the funeral directors are caring and compassionate and reasonable, to that extent will they be respected by the public. I personally have little cause to fault them.

No young person is likely just to wander into a funeral home. Few preplan for their death or the death of a loved one. Death usually finds us very unready. It is a tragic intrusion into what we have come to hold as the normal order of life.

A Grim Joke?

I once saw a television "panel show" on death. The participants were portrayed as corpses, dressed in evening clothes. The moderator kept punching them and asking them to talk. The sound track gave off peals of laughter. It was a grim sort of humor. Certainly there is no dearth of sick jokes about the dead and the dying. Laughter may be a psychological defense: what bothers us will go away if we can laugh at it. Laughter does help to ease the pathway through life. There is a macabre interest in a book or film like *The Loved One*. The film portrayed certain farcical aspects of the funeral industry, yet it was not widely seen. On the other hand, films of vampires and monsters do have shock value, and people do go to see them. We are fascinated with death. It does, in a way, scare us out of our wits. Maybe this is because we know it is inevitable. No one has yet escaped, not even Houdini. Each year his followers gather at his grave, hoping for him to return. So far, he has not managed to pull off what would be the greatest trick of all—to return from the grave.

Open Curiosity

So long as there is life on earth, human beings will be curious about death. Why must we die? Where do we go after we die? Is there life after death? Humans are also concerned with the very process of life that leads us, after much struggle, to the point where we must face death. The new professionals in the field of dying are saying that we need not face it alone; others can assist us. The government acts as a watchdog on the funeral industry. The cost of dying is studied. But much more than money is involved. We have placed man at the center of the universe. The Bible says we have dominion over the earth. Yet for all of us—king and pauper—death has the final word. This is so very difficult to accept. If we can put a man on the moon, why cannot we find a way to conquer death? Man is frustrated because this last frontier—the goal of immortality on earth—has not yet been reached. Each generation gives us another step forward. One by one, the killer diseases are conquered. Yet death, the ultimate destroyer, is still around. Our average life span may advance to age 76, but even though life is lengthened, it does—at some point—end.

Even more terrifying is the vision of the disability of old age. The vigorous and young become crippled and old. We can see what we are likely to become when we visit a nursing home. This may be why the residents of nursing homes have so few visitors: people do not like to face their own mortality. If we could be born old and die young, life might be more pleasant, but such is not human destiny.

So, if we have not yet conquered death, it is natural for us to wonder about what happens next. Elsewhere in this book we have spoken of this subject in some detail. Another aspect of our curiosity is that it is not curiosity alone. There are fear, anger, frustration, and guilt. Death is an affront to the living. Why are we born to die? We turn to the religionists and philosophers. At the same time, we may increasingly consult the "dying professionals"—those who will have special training to help us confront what is yet to be. There will be a financial cost to train and pay such careerists in the field of "death counseling," but if it becomes vital to have such persons, society will find a way to pay them. Death may be the last frontier of science. Until death is conquered, we have to develop the techniques to deal with it and to retain our sanity in the process. Obviously it is a sensitive area. Complaints are leveled against the "death professionals"—be they clergy or funeral directors. The curious mind searches for answers. Meanwhile, in a pragmatic sense, the dead must be buried and the survivors must be comforted. How this is to be accomplished is a source of continuous debate and discussion.

The sociology of America has helped to create our burial customs. They may change slowly. They are not likely to undergo drastic transformation. Few opt for cremation, even though the cost is somewhat less. The majority do not opt for military funerals, even though here as well money is to be saved. Most seem to prefer the standard use of the funeral home and the cemetery of one's religious faith. It is a question whether these practices will vary in the foreseeable future. I have no crystal ball. If we run out of land, cremation may become more acceptable. This is the case in India, where cremation is the norm. It is difficult to predict the future—every prediction is subject to revision. What will happen in the funeral industry is unknown. If less expensive funerals become the demand of the public, I imagine the industry will respond to it. Suffice it to say, for the moment, that funerals tend to reflect one's class and status in life. Unless our sociology and psychology are altered, present burial practices will continue.

Thought Questions

1. Do you think the costs of funerals are excessive?
2. Have you ever met a funeral director?
3. How would you feel about attending a funeral that was held in a home (rather than in a funeral parlor)?
4. How do you feel about "sick jokes" concerning the dead?
5. Do you think "dying counselors" could be helpful to the families of those terminally ill?
6. How do you feel about cremation?

CHAPTER VII

Make Today Count

With modern sophisticated ways to detect cancer, an increasing number of persons know that they have it. The word "cancer" is said in the hushed tones reserved for something that we fear. Modern pathology often detects precancerous conditions. At times, the doctors themselves are unsure whether or not a person has cancer.

I once talked to a woman in a hospital who told me a tale of terror. She had gone to her doctor for a routine examination. He took cell samples of the area of her uterus. The laboratory report said that she had cancer. Her physician advised that she immediately submit to chemotherapy. Her husband suggested that she be examined by another gynecologist. The second doctor also ran tests. His lab said that the cells did not look cancerous. The patient suggested that the two doctors confer with each other. They did, but could not agree. After much discussion, the second doctor recommended a hysterectomy, just to be sure that if there was cancer, it could be caught in time. The woman was confused. She had consulted with two prominent physicians, who could not agree. The most that could be said was that she might have a precancerous condition. When she asked for more definite information, the doctors were vague and uncertain. Is it any wonder that the woman was depressed? When I saw her, it was the day before her scheduled surgery. She said she had been having excessive bleeding. The surgeon was to do a complete hysterectomy, including removal of the ovaries, since if she did have a tendency toward cancer, it could be eliminated. In talking to other women in that wing of the hospital, I soon learned that each physician had a different idea about whether or not to do a partial or complete hysterectomy. The patients themselves were unsure how to react, since different doctors gave conflicting advice. I was amazed to learn that even in the analysis of cell samples in a laboratory one often could not be sure whether one had cancer or was free of it. Apparently "iron-clad foolproof" tests are not to be found in "border-line" cases. It often becomes a question of whom do you trust?

In the case just cited, I also spoke to the husband of the patient. He was furious with the doctors. "Those doctors," he shouted, "one tells me my wife has cancer and the other says she does not have it. Why can't we get a straight answer?" His experience can be multiplied many times over. With all the knowledge and modern techniques, analysis of cancer is not always certain.

Uncertainty breeds fear. The woman I have discussed now has a fear of doctors. She does not know whom or what to believe. When I last saw her, she was leaving the hospital, still complaining of terrible pain. Her doctor told her to go home and assured her that the pain would pass. She may well have wondered if she had been told the truth about her condition.

Tell Me the Truth

We live in times when knowledge is easily gained. It becomes increasingly difficult to fool the person who has cancer. Even when the patient is not told, there is often a slipup. A nurse or an orderly may tell the patient what he or she was not supposed to hear. This leads to "game playing." The patient pretends he does not know what he has. The family enters into light banter. The game of "let's pretend" may last well into the final stages of illness. Each participant feels he did the right thing. The truth is set aside. The family fears the patient will "fall apart" and lose the will to live. The patient, knowing what he has, does not wish to trouble his relatives further. So the game goes on, and both sides are the losers. Most people in the health professions urge honesty and openness. After the first shock of knowing what is wrong, they feel the patient can better handle the situation.

The conspiracy of silence is common. I often wonder if anyone is really fooled. Patients know that they are not improving. They can see their terrible weight loss. They know something is very wrong. So they are given tranquilizers and not told what is the matter.

One wonders if this is fair to the patient? The bulk of scientific thought seems to say it is better—in most cases—to be honest with the person rather than to pretend that he or she will recover completely.

When You Do Know the Truth

Still another problem is how to cope with the knowledge that you *do* have cancer. Your family has not hidden the truth. The doctor has explained the extent of the illness. You have been given a prognosis as to how far the disease has progressed and what your chances for recovery may be. You have had chemotherapy treatments to try to arrest the spread of the disease. The family has followed current medical advice. You have been told. You have a detailed knowledge of your illness. What do you do now?

There is a man named Orville Kelly, who lives in Burlington, Iowa, and who was the subject of a newspaper article.[1] Kelly, aged 45, is the founder of Make Today Count, a national self-help organization for cancer patients. Kelly feels that the worst problem he and others face is emotional. He has received more than 25,000 letters in the two years since he started organizing chapters of Make Today Count. Kelly admits that his organization cannot perform miracles. It relies on plain talk and common sense. He has noted that in our society we have too many irrational fears about incurable illness. Heart disease does not have the same social and psychological stigma that cancer possesses. People talk freely about their heart conditions, but the word cancer is rarely mentioned—even though, say the doctors, one in every four Americans will contract cancer at some time. The adjectives used to describe cancer add to the terror. It is called insidious, sinister, deadly, capricious. We are led to believe that we deal with an unknown killer that strikes without warning. Prominent persons are struck down as well as the poor and the lowly. It is no respecter of persons, whatever their station in life. We fantasize a horrible cancer-induced death. The doctors are often vague when talking to the patient. In truth, they themselves are not sure how fast it will spread, what are the chances for remission, and

---

[1] New York *Times,* Dec. 5, 1976.

what degree of pain it will produce. Americans want to know. We are a people wedded to the clock. There is a time and a place for everything. Cancer is uncertain. It cannot be precisely clocked. It can lunge forward, or it can regress. It can disappear, only to reappear many years later when the victim believes himself to have been cured. It provides a field day for the quacks and charlatans who have a wide-open field. All sorts of potions and medicines are offered. The victims hear always of new doctors who have magical cures.

What can the patient do? He does not wish to go to the faith-healers or soothsayers. He is willing to conform to the standard practices as prescribed by the physician whom he trusts. What then? What happens next? He may find himself cut off from society. Cancer produces a barrier between the living and those who now are considered by some (often by themselves) as being half-dead. The cancer patient may begin to feel detached from reality. He wonders how long he has to live. What will happen to him? Will he die a slow, agonizing death. D. James Arseneau, a member of the steering committee for a chapter of Make Today Count, says, "Cancer is often not painful (if caught early enough, most cancers don't have to reach the painful stage). Disfigurement is rare. Horror stories about treatments are exaggerated. Actually, many people can return to a reasonably functional life." [1] Some doctors point out that the medical profession has painted itself into a corner where cancer is concerned.

Physicians admit that they have no cure for heart disease, diabetes or other diseases. Many diseases are not curable. Therefore, cancer should be looked upon as still another of the so-far incurable illnesses. Heart disease, diabetes, and cancer are usually controllable. For some reason, we expect a cure for cancer. Millions of dollars are given to research institutes. Cancer is perhaps the most feared of all the unconquered diseases that plague humankind.

Your Chances of Living

The life expectancy rate for cancer victims is rising. Cancer treatment is becoming more and more effective. In the same *Times* article, these are the words of the medical establishment: "According

---

[1] New York *Times,* Magazine Section, Dec. 5, 1976.

to the American Cancer Society, in the 1930's fewer than one out of five people with diagnosed cancer were alive after five years. In the 1950's one in four survived, and in the 1970's the figure has improved to one in three. There are now about 3 million people in the United States who are "cured" of cancer (who remain free of the disease after five years). There have been significant advances in the treatment of some cancers, including acute leukemia, melanoma (a skin cancer), and Hodgkin's disease." In the 1980's the rate of cancer "cures" and "remissions" is steadily increasing. Yet many cancer patients are unable to admit that cancer is just another disease. Society, the media, and all the forces of our society have conspired to make it more than just another illness.

Fear, anger, guilt, rage, loneliness, detachment, awareness of death, and symptoms—both physical and mental—are to be associated with the reactions of the cancer patient. In fact, more and more, cancer is termed a "family disease." It has an effect that spreads far beyond the victim. The families suffer terrible anguish. They often do not know how to deal with the member of the family who has cancer. What do you say? What do you avoid saying? How can you cope with the patient's anger and rage at the world?

For every advance that science provides, it raises new problems. The cancer patient's life is prolonged, yet even when this occurs, many psychosocial problems can arise. Cancer care tends to be crisis-oriented. Priorities favor the treatment of physical illness that is more curable. In the article about Orville Kelly, Dr. Jerome Yates observed that diagnosis and treatment are given the highest priority, and not enough thought is given to the quality of survival.

Kelly believes that more must be done to educate the public. He lectures to doctors and nurses about how the cancer patient really feels. He has said, "My wife was sleeping in another room so I wouldn't hear her crying at night. . . . I remember the time at a party when I had a paper cup and everyone else had a glass."

No Easy Answers

Kelly does not seem to feel that cancer patients should look for miracles. If one learns to be compassionate and caring, that in itself is a miracle. The medical community stresses the search for a cure more than the techniques of care. Therefore, it is not surprising that cancer patients have formed groups like Make Today Count. The group works because its members have something very much in common. They can discuss with each other their hopes, fears, agonies, desires, and plans. If a lone cancer patient discusses suicide as an alternative, he is liable to be locked up; but at meetings of Make Today Count a person can talk openly about the type of despair that drives one to consider suicide. The others will not condemn you; they have had similar feelings.

The worries of cancer patients are understandable. Often they are young. They may have families to raise and educate, and they may wonder how their mates will survive when they die. They may feel guilty about dying—for death is often seen as a cop-out, a way to avoid responsibility. At one meeting of Make Today Count, a member named Elizabeth told a touching tale. "We discussed everything," she said of her dying husband. "I'm glad now he's at peace. I was with him when he died. I held him and told him he had suffered long enough and that it was all right to leave me." At MTC meetings, the talk is often of religion. Some are angry with God, but, through discussion, some of the anger dissipates. One patient said that she wished she could stand on a hillside, like the biblical prophet Jeremiah, and scream at God. Others said perhaps we have to forgive God for not taking away the pain and agony.

It is obvious that there is no one solution to the problem of how to deal with one's feelings. Individuals are different. Our thresholds of pain, anger, and fear are not the same. Our needs vary. So far, little has been done in the health field to care for those who have cancer. Health-care professionals are only recently coming to grips with how to talk to the patients. The busy doctors have little time for "small talk." The patient may yearn for comfort and reassurance, to "talk things out"—not once, but many times. Who is to listen? Self-help groups such as MTC are providing some answers. Its members either have cancer or are members of families where there is cancer. MTC trusts the compassion and common sense of its members. It does not glorify death; instead it tries to help its members get the most out of each day of their lives. A philosopher once said that we should live each day as if it were the last day of our life. If we did this, we would not waste time; it would be far too precious a commodity to fritter away. MTC does not provide deeply intellectual answers. It does try to provide a sense of community and to inspire its members to help each other, in this way, making each member of the group stronger. Kelly says that he seeks to make every day count. He loves his family very much. By concentrating on today and making the most of it, destructive thoughts are pushed aside. Worry solves no problems. Constructive action makes life worthwhile. We do not measure the worth of a book by the number of pages; nor do we measure a life by the number of years we have. It is quality and not quantity that is important. A short story can be more fascinating than a long, dull book. A shorter life, lived fully, can be more enriching than a long life without purpose and meaning. The members of MTC seem to live by this idea. They defy death not by worrying about its inevitability, but by resolving to do the most they can with the days that are allotted to them. To live one day at a time is a good lesson for the healthy. For the sick, it is an even more vital concept. Worry solves very little. Despair and fear can lead to depression and self-pity. We have all met persons who wallow in their misfortune. They seem almost to enjoy the terrible things that happen to them. Masochism is not part of the formula for coping with life. Self-pity only makes it more difficult for our families and loved ones.

Waiting for Death

Make Today Count has taught us that just to wait for death is foolish. But there is an even more vital lesson for those of us blessed with good health. We know that cancer patients do want to talk to us about their hopes, dreams, plans, and fears. We should listen to them. We should not turn away from them or change the subject as being too morbid or depressing. They have a genuine need to talk. They must feel that we care, and that we will give them the most valuable of all gifts—the gift of our time to listen and to counsel, to respond, and to care. If we can do this, we will ease their burden considerably. At times, it may be very hard on the nerves. It is natural to wish to escape from them. Few of us really want to hear someone else's sad story. But if we listen and are supportive, they will know that they are not alone.

A listening ear is a powerful tool to do good in the world. Most of the time we are so busy that we scarcely have the time just to sit down and talk to our fellow human beings. The cancer patient—perhaps more than most—needs to know that you find his problem important. Do not shut him out. If there is a wall, it has to be breached. Cancer is a word that carries a taboo. Cancer patients are treated like victims of a horrible plague: we fear that if we get too close to them, we too may catch this awful disease. It has become the nemesis of the 20th century. It inspires too much fear and dread.

If a woman friend has cancer, we cannot treat her as a leper. We must be open and friendly. Legion are the stories of women who have had breast-cancer surgery and live in fear that their husbands will leave them. Our society is so "breast"-oriented that such fears are quite natural. We have become very much like the ancient Greeks, adoring the perfect physical form. This adds to the burden of the cancer patient. Fear of physical disfigurement is a terrible thought, creating dread. If we worship beauty, what of the one who is not beautiful? Yes, there are contemporary ghosts that must be banished. We cannot put cancer in a closet and pretend it does not exist. Death is the final reality. Doctors say that from the day we are born we begin to die. Some illnesses speed up the process. But that is no reason to reject those who are innocent victims of a force that no vaccine can yet prevent.

Make Today Count

To make today count is a good slogan for both the healthy and the sick. More than that, we must really work with and care about those who have difficulty living fully each day. This is part of the challenge of being human.

I visited a patient in a hospital who had gone through major surgery. All of her friends had told her she could expect to have days filled with pain following the operation, but to her pleasant surprise, she had a minimum of discomfort. The hospital provided excellent care, and she had a very smooth recovery period. I looked out of the window of her room at New York Hospital and saw a small tug making its way up the East River; the harbor lights glowed cheerfully. The patient commented on her luck, and, indeed, she was very fortunate. Other patients on the same floor were in agony, yet her own worst fears had not been realized. I had the feeling that now that she was on the road to recovery, she had made a silent vow to make every day truly important.

The gift of health is perhaps the most precious blessing we can have. We tend to abuse ourselves until some life-threatening event comes upon us. Then, it may be too late. We all know people who smoke. They tell you they will stop tomorrow, but tomorrow never seems to come. We have friends who are obese. They stuff themselves with junk food while promising that next week they will go on a diet.

Our body is our most precious possession. While most of its parts can be repaired, not all can be replaced. If we abuse ourselves, it hastens our own demise. Sickness sometimes gives a person greater clarity of vision. We know that our days on earth are limited. Each day does count. It cannot be relived.

We can learn a precious truth from the MTC people. They know how truly vital it is to live fully—one day at a time. They seek to savor the taste of life, to see beauty in the world, to enjoy their mates and their children and their friends. Their eyes are open not only to pain but—even more important—to the preciousness of our world.

When faced with a genuine health crisis, many of the daily little problems tend to shrink in significance. We can see how foolishly we may have quarreled with friends and associates. Our own petty acts appear foolish in the face of debilitating pain and the threat of imminent death. The families of terminally ill persons bear a heavy burden. They know what genuine grief can be. Illness looms like a shadow over even the bravest of families. The MTC people try not to brood over illness. They seek to live as fully as they can. By being creatively busy, they help to lift the clouds of despair. When they do give way to grief, they can share their feelings with others who are similarly situated. They do, indeed, Make Today Count. Can we, if blessed with health, do less?

Bringing Cheer to Others

I once knew a very brave man. Over the years he had developed a cancer that was eating away at his insides. He went through a series of operations, each one to remove another organ in the hope of stopping the spread of the disease. And each succeeding surgery did serve to delay his ultimate death. I frequently visited him at the hospital to cheer him up, and instead, he always made me happy. He always had a lovely smile on his face. He never failed to inquire about my family. His devoted wife kept in close touch with me. The family alternated between living on Long Island and in Florida. Sick as he was, he helped found and organize a Temple in his Florida community. He never lost the zest for life. He never failed to be interested in what was happening to others. Somehow he had mastered a technique that gave him a measure of serenity of spirit in the face of terrible pain. He was determined to live as fully as he could. He had faith in his doctors. Any new medicine or treatment that they wished to try, he quickly said, "That will be fine." He said, "Bob, I hope that they will learn from my case so that others can be spared." I watched his once strong, virile body as it wasted away. He walked erect on his shrunken frame, his weight loss leaving him looking ghostlike. His wife tried to keep up a brave smile. It was not easy for her, or for their grown children. He rejoiced in his grandchildren. He was able to call himself a lucky man because of the good family that did not desert him in his dire years of need. He was not a member of Make Today Count; he died before the group was functioning. Yet he had somehow acquired the best possible attitude toward his condition. His thoughts were always positive and constructive. He never said a harsh word about anyone, and he was quick to defend those who were attacked by silly and malicious gossip. I will never forget his strong handshake, which he maintained until almost the final moments of his life. An avid golfer, he played the game for as long as his strength would permit him to do so. I never knew him to curse the doctors or to blame God for his condition. He had many saintlike qualities.

As a clergyman, I spend many hours visiting patients in hospitals. On almost every floor, you will find what can only be described as a "good angel." There is always one person—very sick—who makes the rounds of other rooms to cheer up fellow sufferers. When Hubert Humphrey underwent cancer surgery in Memorial Hospital in New York City, he was one of these outgoing people who visit fellow patients with words of comfort and cheer. Nurses will tell you about these people. Often they are at death's door themselves, yet, they do their best to bring cheer to others. After their visits, you realize that whatever affliction you have, others are far worse off.

We wonder what gives one person great courage, while others literally fall apart and lose the will to live. No one has found an answer. It may be our genetic makeup. It may have to do with our sociology, how we were raised, and what sort of value system we possess. Perhaps it is something innate—either you have it or you don't. It is similar to the question one might ask of soldiers who go into battle. Why do some stay and fight while others retreat in panic? The human condition is a mystery. If you possess a reservoir of courage, you are truly fortunate.

The human spirit defies explanation. We should be thankful that so many do have the courage to make each day count, even though it be painful to get up to greet the dawn.

A young woman student in a class I was teaching told me of a dear uncle who had passed away. The student came from a divorced home and did not have a close relationship with her father, but her uncle was always there. He gave her courage and strength. He urged her to go to college. Then he was stricken with multiple sclerosis. The disease moved quickly, and almost before he knew it, he was at death's door. She went to see her uncle in the hospital, but he could no longer speak. She told him that she had finally decided to go to college. His eyes sparkled, and he gave a "thumbs up" sign. Shortly after that, he died. Today, whenever she feels blue or discouraged, she remembers her brave uncle. She still can see him clearly in her mind's eye as he virtually crawled up the ramp to get on the train to go to work. He forced himself to go on despite his terrible crippling. This young woman had seen a personal example of great bravery that had affected her life and given her the determination to try. She said, "I know that my uncle is proud of me, wherever he is. He changed my life. I shall always be grateful to him."

The courageous do affect us. Courage begets courage. We learn by what we see. The bravest merit our admiration. Lives have been changed by good role models.

Not every lesson for living is to be found in a book. Personal contact with a brave, suffering soul may do more than anything else to make us aware of what we can do if we develop the will to try. Another student spoke of her father as being a very brave househusband. Felled by illness, he could not work. He did receive a disability pension. His wife got a job, and he stayed at home doing all the household chores. He cheerfully sang as he hung the clothes out on the line. He scolded the five children when they walked with dirty shoes on the kitchen floor that he had just scrubbed. In their home, there was complete role reversal. Yet he was a happy father and husband. He did not complain about his lot in life; he made the best of it. When he finally died, his five children were grown. As my student spoke of her dad, there was a warm glow in her eyes. She had seen a personal example of bravery in her own home. Her dad lived each day as best he could. What more could be asked of anyone?

Thought Questions

1. Would you want to be told the truth if you had cancer?
2. Can you see the value of a group such as Make Today Count?
3. How are the members of MTC able to help each other?
4. Why is cancer looked upon as being so much worse than most other illnesses?
5. Have you ever been a patient in a hospital? How important is the attitude of the doctors and nurses? How did you feel about them?

CHAPTER VIII

The Child and Death

There are times when you may visit a family in mourning where there are young children present. You wonder how best to comfort a child who has lost a parent or grandparent. As a teenager, you might feel at a loss as to what to say or do. If you have some insight into how death affects young persons, it could be helpful.

Body Language

A child cannot discuss death at an adult level. He may feel that his grandpa is now with ghosts because—if he attended the funeral —he may have heard the clergyperson say that the "spirit is now with God." Children have vivid imaginations. A youngster once told me that he visualized the soul as being like Casper the Friendly Ghost, a television character. Youngsters cannot articulate as do their older brothers and sisters. If you visit a home in mourning, you may see the little grandchildren running around furiously; or you may find a six-year-old girl who tries to imitate her deceased grandmother, as she hovers near grandfather trying to be helpful.

Children may assume the role of the deceased parent, and playact at being Mother, if Mother has died. This is not limited to very young persons; often a grown daughter will try to be a mother to her grieving father. People reinforce this image when they say, "Nancy looks and acts just like her mother. She is the image of Mary." If the mother was an excellent hostess, the daughter may seek to greet the friends of the family (after the funeral) in as gracious a way as her mother might have done. Again, this elicits comments such as, "She *is* her mother!" Psychologically, it is almost as if one has transferred to the surviving daughter the virtues of the deceased mother. The sociology of the returning to the home after the funeral is instructive. Body language is expressed by all the participants. Hysterics may be evidenced by the elderly parent who has lost a child. Others hover nearby, offering aid to calm the person in distress. It is not unusual for a parent to faint at the graveside of her child. Consternation and concern are expressed by all present. On rare occasions, a member of a family suffers a heart attack after attending the funeral of a loved one.

Actual body language can be a matter of culture and ethnic background. Some groups, such as Jews and Italians, are openly demonstrative. At funerals, you may see much wailing and waving of arms in despair. Other cultural groups approach death with quietness and reserve, showing a minimum of outward grief. Even as adults have body language, so, too, the children express grief in their own way.

A little boy may frantically run his tricycle into the mourners as they sit in the home. The first reaction might be to think, "What a brat that child is." Yet it may only be a way for the little one to try to get attention. He may not know what is expected of him. If you ask a youngster how he feels about the death of a grandparent, he may answer you with silence. He is too young to articulate his feelings. He may respond by pushing or shoving you. This is the way he conveys his anger. Children become confused. Grandpa was taken away. He may wonder if everyone who goes to a hospital goes there to die. And what is death? Are you going to be living up in the clouds somewhere? If death is a deep sleep, a child may be afraid to go to sleep at night, fearing that he will never wake up. Children do have fantasies about death. They may wonder what happened. Did they do something wrong that caused Grandpa to die? Agitated and unsure, they express through body language their discontent and unhappiness. The entire family is affected. The familiar routine is destroyed. Hordes of people, many of them strangers, come to the house after the funeral. The child is unsure how to act or react. What does a nice little girl do? Should she remain in her room? How shall she act when she sees so many people crying? She wonders what death is all about. She may hear adults verbalizing their own uncertainties about the reality of life after death. Do we just end up in the ground? Is that the termination of everything? The child's discomfort is understandable. If he or she thrashes around in confusion, it is a way of "acting out" grief. We should not be unduly alarmed if a child's conduct seems strange and bizarre.

A wise writer has observed that even delinquent conduct may be a way of acting out grief. Adults may pace the floor aimlessly or wring their hands in despair. We have to recognize that a child's security is threatened. If one grandparent dies, this means the other grandparent can also perish. The finality of death, with all the pain it engenders, is not easily confronted. If it is difficult for adults, how much more so is it for children? They are not aware of the social conventions. Their ego strength is limited. It is tied to that of the family. Few books of funeral etiquette have been written. Children have been taught how to behave at the dinner table. Seldom are they given lessons in how to act in a house of mourning.

Telling the Children

A difficult problem is what to tell the young children. Shall we say that Grandfather has gone away on a long trip? Is it wise to say that Grandmother just went to sleep? Will a child be frightened of going to a hospital if he finds out that his parent died there? How much shall a child be told? Some mourners find a helpful release in countlessly retelling all the details leading up to the death itself. They can quote the exact day, hour, and minute when certain events occurred. It is not unusual for the mourners to speak of the dead person's having had one or two apparently healthy, normal days before dying. Even as a lamp often glows brightly just before it goes out, so, too, do terminally ill persons often receive a brief remission just before death comes. Such ideas are endlessly discussed, often within hearing range of the child. The youngster only perceives bits and pieces of the conversation. What is he or she to believe? The confusion is understandable.

My own inclination is for the parent to be as honest as possible, keeping in mind the emotional maturity of the child. It is not necessary to go into long, wordy explanations. You can answer the child in brief sentences. Factual information may well be all that is wanted. If the child asks about heaven and God, then the parent should answer according to his own beliefs. A parent should not say, "Grandma went to heaven," if he does not believe there is a heaven. Children can sense if we are sincere. We do not lie to them about other matters. We should not invent stories that we think are false. If you honestly believe there is a heaven, then by all means say to the child, "Grandfather has gone to heaven. He will not come back to us, but he still loves us." You can explain much better if you believe in what you say.

If you have to explain death to a younger brother or sister, it would be wise—again—if you have doubts, to express them. Not every question that is asked has an answer. You may wish to say, "I am not sure. I do not know if Grandmother is in heaven." The important thing is how you speak to the child. Give your full and complete attention. Answer to the best of your ability. Do not lie. Be candid and open. Children learn early in life that not every question will draw a full response. Death is among the most difficult of problems.

Philosophers have wrestled with what is called "the ultimate concern" for many centuries. You need not expect, in a moment, to come up with a clear, pat answer. Psychologists believe that children should be told the truth. Some have said that most youngsters have a built-in "lie detector." They can quickly sense a false attitude. If you seek to deceive the child, he may not trust you again. Be honest and truthful. Little white lies can be helpful in some social situations, but death is too serious a matter to be lied about.

Expressing Emotions

We tell adults not to cry loudly during the funeral service. We urge the mourners to dry their eyes and not express grief. We thrust tranquilizers upon them, thinking this will be helpful. Often it has the opposite effect. Persons not used to taking drugs should not be sedated prior to the funeral. Well-meaning friends often foist their own favorite drug on the mourner. What works for one may be harmful to someone else. The latest psychology says it is healthy to express grief. When you feel like crying, cry. When you wish to be silent, do so. Do not feel that you have to please others. You must work through your grief in the manner best suited to your own needs. Crying can be healthy. Giving expression to anger can also be a good outlet. Emotions should not be repressed. If they are, they can appear at a later time and do great damage. A natural response to a boy who has lost his father is to say, "Be brave. Be a man. You are now the head of the house." By saying such things, we in effect place a very heavy burden upon the youngster. How can we expect a ten-year-old to suddenly take the place of his father? He is not mature enough to handle his own feelings; he certainly cannot replace his dad. Children should be allowed to be themselves. The less demanding we are, the better. Unreasonable burdens are to be avoided. Reasonable requests can certainly be voiced. Rather than urging the child to "be a man," it is far better to show empathy. Let the youngster know that you fully realize how difficult the situation is. This will let him speak and cry, if he wishes. Be supportive. Be there when he needs to talk to you. Do not expect him to grow up overnight because his father has died. The same approach should be used with girls. They cannot suddenly become the wife and mother if Mom has died.

Doctor John Bowlby of London says that ". . . each child experiences three phases in the natural grieving process. The first is protest. The child cannot quite believe the person is dead, and he attempts, sometimes angrily, to regain him. The second is pain, despair, and disorganization when the youngster begins to accept the fact that the person who has been loved is really gone forever. Finally there is hope, when the youngster begins to reorganize his life without that person." In his pamphlet "Some Questions and Answers About Your Child and Death," Bowlby's approach makes a great deal of sense. The child's feelings are involved. We must help him work through his grief, even as we try to aid the adults to go through the same process. Beyond the pain, anger, and despair, one will reach the level of hope in the future. Life must go on for the living. We cannot live in the past. Society should not demand that we play a role that is foreign to our natures. Each of us has to be our best self. We cannot become a carbon copy of a dead relative.

When speaking to youngsters, do not be afraid of making them cry. Tears are often a healthy release from tension. It is wrong to avoid discussing the deceased. Usually the mourners want to talk about the dead. Unfortunately, friends often think they are doing a favor by discussing trivia. This is normally not what is required. The child, too, may wish to talk about the nice times she had with Nana. Let the child verbalize. Talk is healthy. It is a catharsis. It is helpful to adults to speak about their feelings, and it is supportive to children, also, to articulate emotions at the level of their competence. Tears can be natural, normal, and therapeutic. There is more cause for concern when a person cannot cry. There are times in life to be happy and cheerful. There are also appropriate times for grief and tears.

Mental health is promoted when you acknowledge the reality of a tragedy. Denial is wrong. It is a lie. It can only create mischief. Do not say, "There, there, you must not cry." It might be better to say, "I feel like crying myself when I realize that your dear grandfather has died." This can lead to sobs, and ultimately to a time when the child will talk to you about his or her feelings. Even antagonistic or negative thoughts about the dead should be expressed. A child may feel it is wrong or sinful to speak ill of the dead. But if a child has anger, let him deal with it openly rather than suppressing it. If it remains bottled up, it can only cause harm. If a child expresses anger against a dead grandparent, you might reply, "Yes, there are times when I can recall being unhappy with Nana." This will show the child that you, too, did not consider Nana to be a saint. If you permit the child to feel and to verbalize, it is far healthier.

Going to the Funeral

A crisis often arises over whether or not the child should go to the funeral. Some parents believe that it is an act of kindness to shield their children from death. On the day of the funeral the youngsters may be spirited away to the home of a friend, often with little or no explanation. Instead of including the child in the grief process, he is left out of it. Sometimes the child is sent away for a few days until the mourning period is over. Even for a young child, this can be psychologically harmful. His mind will fantasize. He will wonder what happened to Nana. Where did she go? We never see her anymore on Sundays. Did I do something to make her angry so that she does not come to visit us? The child's mind creates terrible feelings of guilt and anger. Children should not be barred from participating in the grief process. This does not mean that a child should be held up to Nana and told to kiss her as she is stretched out in a casket. But a youngster should be included in as much of the funeral procedure as he or she is capable of absorbing. This can vary from child to child. My own thought is that by the age of 12 or 13 a child should be able to attend the funeral services in the chapel. Whether or not a child of that age should go to the cemetery to see the casket placed in the ground is another question. The parent is the best judge of the emotional stability of his child. Some children are very grown up at age 12; others are immature and unstable. Some authorities feel that a child as young as age 7 should be encouraged to attend the funeral if he wishes to do so. Some authorities hold that if a child is used to going to religious services by age 7, attendance at a funeral service would be appropriate.

Children should not be shut out of significant events in the life of the family. They are included in birthday parties, vacations, and anniversary celebrations. A family is not to share only the good times. A family is truly strengthened when it goes through adversity as a unit. Children should share in the tragic as well as the joyful events. To exclude them is a tragic mistake. Even a funeral is a sharing process; it should draw the survivors more closely together. But this cannot happen if the child is sent away during the mourning period. A child should be allowed to express his emotions with the family at the time of the funeral. He should not be denied such an experience. The child wants to belong. He needs to give and receive the warmth of love and caring that surfaces during a crisis. It can be damaging to his emotional development to exclude him from the sorrows of life. Life is with people, be it in happy times or in difficult moments.

The Rituals of Death

Each faith provides a way to work through one's grief. There is the preparation for the funeral and the visits to the funeral home. The words of the clergyperson are spoken. The casket is conveyed to the cemetery. It might be wise to explain to a child what to expect before you take him to a funeral service. Try to put him at ease, so that he can better accept what will happen at the funeral home or at the graveside. Some have suggested that on an initial visit to the funeral home the child should go only with a few close relatives. This may make it easier for him to verbalize his feelings and ask questions.

The behavior of an older brother or sister can be helpful to the young child. If you panic, the youngster may react with fear and alarm. If you are calm and mature, the child will model his or her conduct after yours. If you must cry, explain to the child why you are crying, allowing your sibling to feel included in your circle of love and perhaps also to cry. Shared grief is normal to the process of mourning. It should not be stifled.

Love and Death

It may seem strange to group the words "love" and "death" together, yet they are related. The love you give to a child will enhance his sense of security and well-being. He will not feel that he is left outside the circle of your concern. Love is supportive. It is needed in full measure when death intrudes into the family. Do not be afraid to be demonstrative. A friendly arm around the shoulder of a confused little girl may do more good than a thousand spoken words. Your body language can express the compassion that you feel. Support and reassurance are needed. A child who sees a father die may wonder, "Who will take care of me if mother also dies?" Then, having had such a thought, the child may feel guilty for even thinking it. In actuality, such a thought is perfectly natural. We all need someone to care for us. Children know that they need their parents. If one dies, it is normal for them to worry about themselves. They can visualize a different kind of world where they have only one parent. Dad will not be here to take me to the ball game. Or, mother will not be around to cook our meals. How will we be fed? Will I get a new mother or father? The thought of wanting a new parent can induce unconscious feelings of guilt, yet to desire to replace the dead parent is perfectly natural. A child must be allowed to talk about such matters, so that they can be brought to the surface. The child must be made to see that such ideas are not sinful. They are the expected reaction when we suffer the loss of one near and dear to us.

Remember, it is not sufficient just to talk to the child. You must give the child ample opportunity to talk to you. Let the girl express her thoughts of love. Let her wonder about rejection. She may feel guilty, thinking that Daddy purposely went away because he did not love her. She may fantasize that she caused his death by being naughty. She must be made to know that Daddy does not hate her; she did not cause his death. Dad was sick. The doctors did everything they could, but sometimes even the doctors cannot save us. Most of us will live long, productive lives, but, unfortunately, some persons do die when they are young. They do not die because they want to leave the family. Death is not an escape. It does not mean the dead stopped loving us, nor does it imply that if we had loved them more and been better, they would now be alive. The child can be beset by fears. If you offer chances for the little girl to talk, eventually she will. Do not be discouraged if, upon hearing of the death, the words do not tumble out. The child may wish to talk about it at the most unexpected moments. You may be sitting at the dinner table when the child asks, "Where is Nana now?" You should be prepared to give an answer. Tell the youngster what you feel in your heart. Trust yourself. There are few pat answers to be found in the greatest books of wisdom. It is said of King Solomon in the Bible that God offered him any gift under the sun. Solomon said to God, "Give me an understanding heart, and everything else will fall into place." There is much truth in such a notion. Those who are truly wise are to be envied. If you avoid panic and answer with sincerity, you are being helpful.

It helps just to let the child ventilate his feelings. He will soon begin to find answers that work for him. Do not shame the child. Do not criticize him if what he says about the dead sounds strange. It is his way of understanding the situation. His way is not your way. He can only react within the framework of his own maturity (or lack of it). It is not a question of being right or wrong. Children are not little adults. Children are children. They behave according to their physical age and mental development. We should not expect them to be otherwise. Criticism or condemnation are out of place. Sympathy, understanding, and openness are the keys to unlock the heart and bring relief. Your love will be evident, even if you say nothing. The love you express through body language will say even more than words. You do not have to worry about being articulate. Being present and giving the child a chance to speak will do wonders. And, if possible, do not work through your own grief feelings entirely with the child. Do not make the child a substitute for the deceased. The child is his own person. It is vital to respect the integrity of the child. He has his own thoughts, personality, feelings, and desires. A good listener is vitally needed.

Psychologists have pointed out that we communicate what we are in many ways. Our fears, frustrations, and desires are at a conscious and an unconscious level. Children sense how we feel. Our words may say one thing, but the expression on our faces may say something else. Children are aware. They recognize and respect our honesty. It is not a sign of our failure if a child has a need to speak to a clergyperson. Such a person may be able to clear up many misunderstandings. The clergyperson can explain the rituals and symbols of the funeral service, talk to the child about God, and explain away the fears a child might have concerning a deity who brings death to human beings.

If basic theology is needed, by all means talk things over with your cleric. The clergy have extensive experience in helping people of all ages to cope with grief. It is never a sign of weakness to turn to others for help. Many clerics look upon their congregation as an extended family. They may know of excellent persons in the health profession who can be of assistance. Facing death is a communal effort. Every resource should be mobilized to be supportive to the family, and especially to the children.

As soon as possible, the children should be returned to a normal routine of public and religious schooling. It is important that the normal duties and chores of daily living be resumed with due and deliberate speed. Mourning should not be endless. The living must return to the world of everyday life. A child should not be allowed to retreat into memories of the past. During the mourning period, the family will discuss and relive in their minds the years spent with the deceased. It is healthy to go through this period of "instant replay" of the past. But to dwell on it endlessly is not healthy. You must not let the past ensnare you. Life is to be lived, each day.

The family must move ahead and face each new experience with as much courage, laughter, and bravery as can be mustered. The child must be caught up in a renewed sense of being loved. At the same time, he takes his place in the changed circumstances of the family. Routines may have to be readjusted. In time, he may have to get used to having a new father or mother, or new siblings. All of that can wait for the developing future. Time cannot be hurried. Man's capacity for adjustment is shown time and time again. Life means change. The child becomes an adult. In time, he or she will marry and embark upon raising a family. Maturity comes as we grow and develop. The child is the father of the man, as the poet expressed it. But the love and support we give the child today will help him or her to develop into a mature adult tomorrow.

Trust Yourself

When dealing with the problem of death, you should realize that there are few experts. We are in the realm of feeling. If something feels right and true, then do it. Books can suggest ideas. Volumes have been written about death, based on the experiences of others. A work such as *Widow* by Lynn Caine can provide some insights. Yet even the best-written book reflects only the experiences and feelings of the author.

No two persons react to death in quite the same way. Your feelings when you enter a funeral home for the first time may differ greatly from the reactions of your best friend. It is the same in many areas of life. No two persons have exactly the same fingerprints. Our emotional fingerprints vary also. Our ability to absorb stress differs. Some have a greater capacity for love. Some persons make excellent social workers, others are adapted to be competent administrators. A man may be an excellent surgeon yet exhibit limited empathy toward his patients. He can be an excellent technician and be weak in the area of human relations.

The variations of human response are limitless. Shakespeare said, "To thine ownself be true, / And it must follow, as the night the day, / Thou canst not then be false to any man." There is great wisdom in these words. If you are truly your best self, your reactions will be correct. It cannot be stressed often enough how vital it is to let your feelings of care and concern shine through. Ventilate your feelings. Do not be afraid to articulate your own fears, frustrations, angers, and hostility. At the same time, speak of your love. Death must be faced at several different levels. There is the personal, gut reaction, involving how you truly feel. You may be genuinely angry with the dead. You may have hated him in life. Death does not turn one into an angel.

One cleric remarked, half in jest, that he never officiated at the funeral of a sinner. Death does soften our hates. We do tend to see the virtues of the dead. But if residual anger remains, it may be very wise to speak of it. Beyond your own feelings about the dead are the support and comfort you can give to the survivors. Here, you can be of great aid. As a teenager, you are closer to the child who has suffered the loss. Youth will often respond best to youth. Young people live in their own world. They tend to shape and fashion their own subculture. So you may have the right words—spoken in the language of your contemporaries—to be of great help to a family where there are young children who have suffered a loss.

Can you really trust your own feelings? Do so, by all means. You will make some mistakes. It is human to have flaws. It is not what you say; it may well be how you say it. The sincerity of your voice can bring comfort to a broken heart. Just being there—even being with others during long silences broken only by sobs—can be healing to the young mourner who may feel terribly alone and rejected. Life is with people. The mourners need time to be alone, but they also need even more time with others. The mourning period is the time to share one's thoughts, memories, hurts, and empathy.

Reaching Maturity

Maturity is not a gift. We have to work to attain it. You can be mature at almost any stage or age of life if you live up to your physical and emotional capacities. Little children can be quite mature if given the chance. Let the child "act out" his or her feelings. He will respond at his own level of expression. I have seen little children who reach out and comfort their grieving parents. They do this without being prompted. Maybe it is instinctive, or maybe they are just imitating other adults.

Death has many terrible implications. Family life is disrupted. Life-styles can be altered. Change occurs when it is not sought or wanted. A rupture takes place. The breach must be healed. Every death leaves emotional scars. It takes time for healing to be effective.

How can one find the path to maturity? Death may force us to grow up a bit more quickly. We may be forced to assume responsibilities we did not feel we were ready to undertake. The strong are able to respond to new pressures. The body is amazingly resilient. We have marvelous powers of recuperation.

Most of us can stand the physical shock of surgery to our bodies. In time, we return to normal life. Death is a shock to our emotional system. It can also affect our physical selves. The truly mature individual can weather the storms. Each of us captains his own ship of destiny in this world. We will have days of smooth sailing but also times when storms rage. Others may look to us for safety, for a haven. The young may turn to you because you are also young. You can share their doubts and fears and relieve their anxious moments. It is a remarkable challenge. Youth has powers—vast, and often untouched.

A young woman, a freshman in an upstate New York college, told me recently of a volunteer project in which she and a friend are engaged. They are working with two young children who have learning disabilities. The young woman's eyes glowed as she said it was the most exciting project she had ever undertaken. She found she was breaking through in working with a child who was both autistic and hysterical. The youngster could not speak but was really trying. As a young person herself, she could relate to this five-year-old. I have no doubt that she will succeed in her task. She approaches life with great enthusiasm and hopes, in time, to be of service to others. She may eventually wish to work with disadvantaged children, as a trained teacher. As we spoke, I could tell that she was working with a minimum of guidance. She had reached a level of maturity where she had learned to trust her own feelings. At the age of 18, she possessed more maturity and poise than many persons twice her age. Maturity is not only a question of how old you are, but of who you are. Empathy can be a natural gift. It can also, I believe, be cultivated.

Never be afraid to reach out to those who need help. When death comes, it is vital to share one's grief. Today, you are aiding someone else. Tomorrow, others may comfort you. No one escapes from the reality of death. If we develop courage, then maturity follows. Look around you. When you least expect it, you may have the chance to be helpful to a little child looking for a friendly hand to hold. Let it be yours. The experience will enrich and mature you. It will make you aware of how much we need one another in our journey through life.

Thought Questions

1. How do you think a child really feels when a parent dies?
2. What do we mean by "body language"?
3. How honest should we be in telling a child about death?
4. Do you think the clergyperson or doctor can be helpful when there is a death in the family? In what ways?
5. How do you feel about mourners who do not cry at a funeral?
6. Should children ever be forced to attend a funeral?
7. How would you feel about explaining death to a child?

CHAPTER IX

AIDS—What to Do?

It is in the newspapers every day. Talented young artist is struck down in his prime. Schoolchild is shunned by classmates. Family is forced to leave the community. Over and over again we read about AIDS (acquired immunodeficiency syndrome).

By 1986 the disease had spread to seventy-eight countries. By 1988 it was being reported in almost every country on earth. A research organization in London has predicted that in the next decade one million people in Africa will die of the disease. At a 1987 Conference on AIDS in Washington, D.C., Dr. Jonathan Mann estimated that 5 to 10 million people in the world are already infected with the AIDS virus, and one million or more active cases could emerge worldwide by 1991. At that same conference it was estimated that in the United States one in every thirty males between the ages of twenty and fifty was infected. An AIDS "hot spot" is the New York–New Jersey area, where currently it is estimated that 200,000 or more intravenous drug users have AIDS.

Homosexual men and intravenous drug users account for nine out of ten cases in America. Each day on television and radio and in the press, warnings are given. We hear about "safe sex" and "clean needles" and "Say no to premarital sex." Learned physicians and other public health workers appear on the TV talk shows, engaged in earnest discussion about what to do. AIDS has arrived. At the moment no cure or immunization is in sight. We read of young, upwardly mobile men (since men seem to be the most likely victims) who are cut down in the prime of life. Big-city obituary columns are filled with the tragic stories of those taken too soon from this life.

We know that the world has had terrible plagues from time to time. In the Middle Ages the bubonic plague killed half the inhabitants of Europe during a two-hundred-year period. Then that plague returned for fifty more years of destruction.

With all the capabilities of modern research, a cure for AIDS is still years away. Immunization is not yet possible. Education seems to be the key, to teach those at highest risk to avoid this fatal infection. The drug culture and the former easy and open sex life with multiple partners—as found in the gay community—contributed to its spread. An AIDS patient declares, "Sitting on a time bomb. Living under the gun. Waiting for the other shoe to drop."[1]

Your Reaction

It is quite possible that you will encounter an AIDS patient in your school. In all likelihood he or she has leukemia and contracted AIDS through a blood transfusion. Or the person might be an intravenous drug user who has been sharing a needle with a friend. What can you do?

Many people shun the AIDS victim. Often he feels isolated. In some cases his family make it clear that he is not welcome in the home. Friends may disappear, fearing that in being near him they may catch the disease. Even though the medical community has stated that "casual contact" does not transmit AIDS, many remain fearful. The AIDS patient feels like a leper, shunned by society. In hospitals, the staff often wear special gloves and masks when entering his room. He may long desperately for some human, caring contact, but AIDS counselors are in short supply.

If a friend is stricken, your continued friendship can ease his final days of life. Just being there for him will make a great difference. Some AIDS patients practice denial. They pretend that they are not sick. Others put up a good front. They act macho and say, "I will beat this thing." Then there are those who fall into deep depression and become suicidal. The world looks bleak. They feel there is no hope.

I can recall in vivid detail a visit I made to a young man who had AIDS. I told him that I had that day heard a report on the radio about a new drug that was showing promising results. He looked me in the eye and said, "Every day you hear about something that may work. But it is always untried and will not be ready for use on humans for several years. It will not help me. It is too late for me and my generation." This was said very matter-of-factly by a young man who knew his days on earth were limited.

He was one of the lucky ones. His family sheltered and loved him to

---

[1]*Someone Was Here*, by George Whitmore. New American Library, New York, 1988.

the end of his days. His lover visited him from time to time. Others are not so lucky. They may lose their job, have their insurance canceled, and be evicted from their apartment by a fearful landlord.

As the immune system breaks down, the AIDS victim often suffers a debilitating, painful period leading to death. Seeing others suffer and knowing what is in store for him does not help. Support groups are vital to help him face the inevitable.

Why Me?

AIDS patients often say, "Why did this happen to me? I am too young to die. My life has barely begun. It is just not fair." Counseling such persons is extremely difficult. However, if you have a friend who is stricken and you keep in touch and are helpful, you are indeed being of great comfort.

AIDS counselors often find that their clients are not responsive and become angry and frustrated. This is to be expected. As they walk down the street they see others who are feeling fine while they know that at any moment they may have to be rushed to a hospital. Some have called it a "living death."

A Future Cure?

Until a cure is found, some things can be done. Every effort should be made to let the AIDS victim know that he is not alone, that there are people who are concerned. Do not be frightened and run if the person is rude to you. He may be testing you, to see if you really care. He may be going through a denial stage, and you are a reminder to him that he has AIDS. But if you persevere, if you "hang in there" and do not give up, the chances are that your stricken friend will be truly grateful and will turn to you as someone who did not reject him. AIDS is a disease. The person who has it is still a person, even though he has a fatal illness. Respect the personhood of those who have contracted the virus. And—practice safe sex. Avoid the drug scene, and be wary of those IV drug users who share needles. While there is no cure for AIDS, there are sensible precautions to be taken to avoid infection. In 1988 an eight-page booklet on AIDS was mailed to every American household. The government is aware of the urgent need for both education about AIDS and scientific research to defeat this emerging plague.

What Else Can You Do?

If a friend dies of AIDS, try to comfort the family. They will appreciate your visiting them. The families of AIDS patients also need help in coping. Until a cure is found, people must band together to reach out to those who are stricken. The death of the young from this incurable virus is a daily, ongoing tragedy. You can be a good neighbor and friend. Until an effective immunization and cure are available, our life-styles must change. Multiple sex partners are bad news. Sharing needles can be fatal. Safe sex is a must. Only the foolish would risk their lives in today's world, where AIDS cases continue to multiply at a frightening rate.

Thought Questions

1. How important is it to keep up with the latest information about AIDS?
2. Have you ever spoken to an AIDS victim? Do they seem to be "different" from other people? Why?
3. Do the media overdo in trying to frighten the public about AIDS?
4. Does AIDS education belong in the school, or in the home, or in the media? Can the school, home, and media work together to keep the public informed?
5. Should the AIDS epidemic influence you to change your life-style?
6. Do you think there will ever be a cure for AIDS? Why, or why not?
7. Should obituaries of AIDS victims state how the person died?
8. Does the death of celebrities such as Rock Hudson or Liberace make people more sympathetic to those who have AIDS?

CHAPTER X

Religion's Answers

Religions do not deny the reality of death. If you are troubled about dying, you may find your way to your clergyperson. Ministers deal with the problems of death and dying on a daily basis. As America grows older, more and more of us will live to a ripe old age, but we eventually will pass from this world. The clergyperson can add an extra dimension to helping you grope with the problem. Each religion has some words of comfort. It is true that some fundamentalist faiths speak of hellfire and eternal damnation. Yet this is not the main thrust of most religious thought. Whether or not you are a literalist where the Bible is concerned, the chances are that you will find help in your faith when coping with death.

What Do I Do?

After a family is informed by the doctor of the death of a loved one, the next person usually summoned is the clergyperson. For those affiliated with a church or synagogue, the natural response is to call your minister, priest, or rabbi. If you do not have affiliation, you probably know of someone who does. The clergy help the family to make the arrangements with a local funeral director. The clergyperson is with you, to be of comfort and to answer questions. Do not feel embarrassed to ask about the proper procedure for a funeral in your faith. Burial customs do vary. You will work out whatever procedures and practices are best suited to your needs. Often, the cleric will meet with you, either at your home or in the funeral parlor, before the funeral itself. If the clergyperson knows the family, it will make it easier for him to conduct the funeral service. If he does not know the deceased, he will build his eulogy around what members of the family tell him. Sometimes a member of the family may wish to speak at the funeral ceremony, which adds a personal touch to the proceedings. Occasionally, I have seen teenagers speak at a funeral, or, they may give the clergyperson a poem or an essay about the deceased. Anything that can personalize the service will add to its significance. What is said by those who knew the individual is truly the most meaningful.

Recently, I officiated at a funeral for an 85-year-old woman. Her middle-aged son, a psychiatrist, asked me if he could say a few words about "Mom." As he spoke, tears came to his eyes. Those in attendance were deeply moved. He was far more eloquent and direct than I could have been. It was *his* mother. He loved her. He was able to articulate his thoughts. It was good for him to do this, and healthy for the congregation to hear him.

Do not hesitate to talk things over with your pastor. You will find him (or her) to be very sympathetic. Most are closely "tuned in" to your thoughts and emotions. The clergy devote much time to visiting the sick and ministering to the dying. They can be of enormous help, if they are approached.

The Role of the Clergy

The mourner may feel guilty that he was not more attentive and helpful to the deceased. You may deeply regret that at times you were unkind to the one who is now gone. Talk about your feelings to your pastor. Tell him of your emotions of guilt, anger, and frustration. It is healthy to "talk things out." The clergyperson has a trained, listening ear. He is one of the few people who will not rush you out of his office. He looks upon the ministry as containing a viable pastoral thrust. If your guilt feelings are of a religious nature, then surely speak to him. For example, you may wish to question him about the whole idea of heaven and hell. Or you may wonder about the reality of the human soul. I have been asked, "Rabbi, will I ever see my mother again?" Since I believe in the immortality of the soul, it was easy for me to give an affirmative reply.

After talking to your minister, you will probably discover that your guilt feelings are unfounded. Seldom is there a death that does not arouse emotions of "guilt." Even with those who say they have nothing to feel guilty about, the very fact that they feel they have to say it shows that it is still on their minds. Real guilt can exist but, nonrational guilt creates ongoing problems. You cannot confront the dead; therefore, it is good to "talk through" your feelings. The clergy exist to help people. You are a person. It is very natural to turn to your pastor.

Theological Problems

The word "theology" means "ideas about God." When death comes, we often question the deity. Many times you hear people say, "Why did he die so young? He was a good man." The most difficult part of the pastor's duties is to comfort a family where a young child or a young parent has died. There is a terrible sense of despair. The death is useless. It serves no purpose. Parents are heartbroken and tend to personalize the event. They feel they are being punished. The biblical story of Job speaks of the problem of the righteous who suffer. The good are not always rewarded with long, happy lives. The saying, "The good die young" is more than a cliché. You may have been concerned about this. Religion may not have all the answers, but some replies can be given.

Where Is God?

The bereaved often ask, "How can a good God kill someone so nice, so needed?" Religion says that it is not God that destroys us. Each person, from the moment of birth, begins to die. Some of us are born with healthier and stronger bodies and are able to fight off disease. We may be among the lucky ones who will live to a ripe old age. It is not a question of whether you are good or bad. It is whether or not you are blessed with a strong constitution that resists disease. Some people drive themselves without mercy and still live to a ripe old age. Some persons drink heavily and dissipate but do not pay the price. There are also quiet, kind persons who do not submit to overly stressful situations—yet they die young. Some have vigor and well-being well into their 90's; others wither in their 40's.

It is not that God is absent. What is involved is the fact that God does not intervene in human nature. Most Western religions say that since the days of the Bible God does not talk directly to us. "God moves in a mysterious way his wonders to perform." How God acts is largely a mystery. Christians hold that when the Messiah returns to earth all souls will stand in judgment. When will this occur? Christian theologians are not sure. In traditional Judaism are the words, "though the Messiah tarry, I will wait for him." For Jews, the Messiah is to bring about an age of peace, when the dead will experience resurrection. Again, there is no certainty when this will occur. The point is, in Western faith, there is no answer as to why some die young and some do not. This will be revealed to us after we die. Those who know the truth are the dead themselves. They have become part of God's kingdom. This is what much of Western religious thought seems to be saying.

If you ask, "Where is God?", the pastor will reply, "God is everywhere." Then you may question why a certain person dies: "Is this the will of God?" No, it is not the will of God that you should die at a particular moment. Most Western religions are not fatalistic. We are told to fight against death, and to postpone it by every reasonable means. The Bible does say in Ecclesiastes: "A time to be born, and a time to die." But the Bible does not say when this will occur. How is God active in the process? Here is the mystery. No clergyperson has a complete answer.

A Better Life Coming?

The Catholic Church does teach that the next world will be better than this one. Religions that speak this way do offer a full measure of comfort to the mourners. Judaism also has a concept of the world to come, but most Jews place great stress on remaining alive in this world. There is uncertainty as to what is to be found beyond our experience here.

The Old Testament speaks of the dead as being asleep. Other biblical passages assign the dead to a place under the ground, called Sheol. Judaism declares that the dead will one day arise. Traditional Jewish thought speaks of a Divine deliverer called the Messiah. When the dead arise, the souls will be reunited with the bodies. Then they will stand in judgment before the throne of God. The Messiah will lead each person to the heavenly throne. At that time, an accounting will be made.

In truth, most religions of the Western world do deal with the immortality of the soul. Words such as "soul" or "spirit" are utilized. Christianity speaks of resurrection with great seriousness. This will occur when the rejected Messiah again returns to this earth, to redeem the world. A general theme in Western religious thought is that "the dead shall live," but the exact form of life is vague. One rabbi envisioned a large table in heaven, where the male souls sat around studying the holy books, while the female souls sat and listened to their discourses and discussions. This was a rather sexist view of heaven!

It is important to emphasize that our Western religious heritage sees a survival beyond the grave. There is a type of life for the soul (possibly united with the body) in the world that is yet to be.

Christian theology speaks of a purgatory, where souls go to be cleansed before they are admitted to heaven. In Jewish thought, we find the idea that the souls return directly to God. Few of the rabbis envisioned a purgatory for the evil soul. In the Talmud, a book of Jewish law and lore, it was felt that only the generation living in the days of the biblical Noah would be consigned to eternal damnation.

Eastern religions move in a somewhat different direction. They hold that we are all part of nature. After death, there is a continuation in nature. Some Eastern religions speak of the transmigration of the soul. They believe it possible to be reborn more than once. Some speak of a cycle of seven rebirths of each soul before it is finally at peace. In Hindu thought, the cow is sacred. It might house the soul of a long-dead ancestor.

What to Believe?

There are many religions. Each of them tries to bring comfort in tragic times. If you have been reared to believe that God is love, how can a loving God take someone away from you? Actually, the person is not gone. Religions say that the physical being is placed in the earth, but the spirit or soul lives in another place, with God. Are the dead really far from us? If you lose someone you truly love, you will never forget that person. Parents who lose a child have said that they think about the child almost every day of their lives. Somewhere in the back of our minds, we remember the person. In time, the memories tend to fade. This can be healthy. To live only in the past creates problems. You may be more comfortable in not facing the future; but eventually we must spend most of our time in the world of the living. We function in the here and now.

Do the Dead Speak to Us?

I believe that, in a way, the dead do speak to us. We cannot communicate with them face to face; yet as we remember them, we think of what they would expect of us. If your parent dies, this is not the end of the relationship. Each day you may wonder, "Would my dad be proud of me if I did this or that?" "What would my mother say if she knew I made that decision?" We may not consciously talk to the dead, but in a real sense they never leave us. Psychologists say that the influence of the parents is so great that even when they have been dead for many years, we still want to please them.

Most religions accept the finality of death. After you draw your last breath, your earthly presence becomes nil. Some people go to mediums to establish contact with the dead. Mediums flourish especially after wars, when there is much eagerness to talk to those slain in battle. Most have little faith in such an approach. I have known of persons who do talk to the dead, going to the cemetery and talking at the grave site. Actually, such a person is really talking to herself or himself, trying to determine what the beloved would counsel.

Uncertainty About Life After Death?

If you have ambivalent feelings about life after death, you have a great deal of company. It is not unusual to believe one day and to be skeptical the next. The human mind is not constant. It grows and develops. The longer you live, the more new experiences you will have. What happens to you—your life-style, friends, teachers, and—above all—your own experiences will shape your thinking. Freud speaks of the superego—the conscience—which controls ideas of right and wrong. It is possible that your superego may move you toward believing in a God who knows what is right and what is wrong. With faith in God, you may move quite naturally to faith in a future world, where the wrongs of this life are righted. Some religions teach that the righteous will receive the rewards they were denied in this life. The world-to-come can be seen as an attractive place where the records are set straight. The concept of heaven and hell was an attempt to conceptualize such a Divine setting for re-ordering matters. Also, it was thought that man might be more likely to behave if an eventual accounting would take place.

The Function of Religion

Religion can be of service. Spiritual matters are a part of life for most of us. We seek to develop a value system. Much of what we believe is acquired through what we experience and what we learn. The sacred books of religion record what others have felt and sensed about life. If you find certain teachings valid, they can serve to guide you in your daily life. Psychologists tell us that persons of deep faith are better able to accept death. If your faith offers a promise that "death is not the end," you may be able to relax a bit more. If tragedy strikes, you will find comfort in the thought that you will have contact with your loved one in a future life. However, if you are skeptical about life after death, even here religion can be of service. Pastors do a lot of listening. They exist to serve and to counsel. Few will impose their ideas upon you. Do not hesitate to see your minister, even if it has been a long time since you attended a religious service. Most ministers today are not in the business of "condemning" those who have strayed from the church or synagogue. They can be helpful if you let them, and, as you discuss things, you may gain some new insights and answers. Religion deals with the eternal "why" questions of life. It cannot hurt at least to gain some insight from your pastor.

If you do not believe in immortality, you will find that some clergypersons also went through periods of doubt. Not to believe with perfect trust is far more common than one might think.

The Answer?

Is there one right answer for all of us? I do not think so. Each of us is a person with our own individual experiences. Some accept the reality of death and do not look to God as being heartless and cruel. Such people can say that God moves in mysterious ways, His wonders to perform. So, we should not question Him. Others become very angry at the apparent cruelty of death; in fact, tragedy may destroy their faith. Most will be somewhat confused about it. Then, as the dark clouds of mourning gradually give way to a bit of sunshine, they will find ways to cope with death and go on. The most that religion can do is to suggest a path to follow. If it makes sense to you, you will be comforted. If it does not, you will search for other ideas. Death has a numbing effect on us. Our emotions become jumbled. We are angry one moment and calm the next. We can accept the reality of death, then a few moments later cry, "It cannot be true." The survivor may act punch-drunk, like a boxer who has received a tremendous blow to the head. He may stagger, mentally, and be very much in a fog. The wounds do heal, but the scars remain. The memories are not erased. They stay with us—probably for a lifetime.

Breaking Away?

Children dream of someday being free of parental control. Psychologists hold that we never completely free ourselves of the influence of our families—especially our parents. We grow up, marry, and move away. Yet the ties with our origins continually assert themselves. So, when a parent dies, we are not completely orphaned. It is true that the physical presence is gone, but our memory banks and our emotion systems are still filled with feelings about the dead. So we do not break away, even if we want to. The feelings—good and bad—stay with us. Something in our unconscious will draw us back to memories and events that we thought we had lost or set aside.

We live at the conscious level of being. Life is with people. The living relate to the living. Still, the dead are carried within us. So, in a way, they never die. Something of them remains a part of us. If the dead have too strong a hold on us, it is time to seek psychiatric help; but if we can put the memory of them into proper perspective and focus, we can lead fairly normal lives.

Most religions afford specific times to offer prayers for the dead. This can be a time of healthy release. At memorial services, people often cry. There is nothing wrong with expressing your feelings. However, if you experience excessive grief for an extended period of time, you should have counseling. The point is, the funeral does not end the relationship. The dead do not completely disappear. We visit the grave and see the stone. We are aware that they are in the earth. It may frighten us. We may be very leery about going to a cemetery. Fear is a natural reaction. All of us have some fright about the unknown. Death is shrouded in mystery. Few can approach it in a matter-of-fact way. Even clergypersons, who work with mourners on an ongoing basis, have problems with their own feelings. Never think that you are the only one to wrestle with how to relate to death and dying. It is a universal problem. It cries out for more light and love. There are few experiences you will have that others have not had. Many of the things we do follow a universal pattern. The Bible says, "There is nothing new under the sun." Actually many new things occur, but in the area of emotions there is much repetition. We can learn from the experiences of others, yet so much of life is self-discovery. No one can teach you how to feel when a loved one dies. You just react. Your emotions take over. You may sob or be still. You may pace restlessly. You may become irritable and irrational. You may be calm and comforting to others. It is like going into battle. No commander can be sure which of his soldiers will be brave and which will turn and run.

Some Personal Thoughts

As a clergyman, I have to deal with my own feelings and emotions. When a teenager dies, usually many of his friends come to the funeral chapel. They look so defenseless and confused. Young people tend to think that death is far removed; when a contemporary dies, they are deeply shaken. They cry not only for their friend. They cry also for themselves. They now know that it *can* happen to them. The young do not wish to die. It is natural to feel that the old should go first. Your entire life is ahead of you—there is so much to do. The youngster who dies creates all sorts of tensions and feelings in the family. Parents may grieve the rest of their lives. Sometimes the strain of a young death can destroy a marriage. Often the brothers and sisters of the deceased suffer terribly. They may unconsciously feel that they were partially to blame for the death. All sorts of emotions rise to the surface when the shock of death reaches your nervous system.

In my work as a pastor, I have seen that the death of a young person is like a pebble dropped into water. It radiates ripples in many directions. The impact is one of shock and dismay. Parents cry out, "What went wrong? Why did it happen?"

Our generation is especially vulnerable. We see death recorded on the evening news; it is glorified in television dramas. When it actually happens to one you love, you are no longer a spectator. You do not just watch others suffer; now the hurt is your very own. Your defenses are there to shore you up, but you are also very vulnerable.

If you have had doubts about religion, when death strikes you may become an agnostic. "There cannot be a God if this can happen." Death upsets the accepted order. Our society is geared to being born, living a long life, and dying in peace. This is the anticipated scenario—our fantasy—but it is not always reality. No life moves smoothly. Few can live without pain and frustration. Life fluctuates between good days of fulfillment and difficult days of sadness. Fortunately, most of us have a reasonable chance of living long, productive lives. With a bit of luck and effort, we can utilize our intelligence to make something of ourselves. When death strikes a bright, promising youngster, it is almost impossible to accept. Our sense of order is thrown out of gear.

I have seen many who thrash around after the death of a loved one; others are able to remain calm. Some, when they lose a child, begin to do volunteer work on the children's floor of a hospital, to comfort others who are suffering. You can never be sure how you will act or react. When the young are dying, the families often seek a pastor to pray with them. Prayers cannot insure a miracle. Religions teach that God seldom intervenes directly in the affairs of men. If he did so, He would upset the laws of nature.

Go Forward

All of life is "moving on." When I counsel mourners I point out that all we really have is today and tomorrow. We cannot bring back yesterday. We cannot relive happy times except in our memories. And we certainly do that. Mourning is often "instant replay," as families talk about events of years gone by. This is fine, so long as you do not remain in the nostalgia mood forever.

In this world, we go forward from one experience to another. It is not healthy to dwell too long on the past. It serves no constructive purpose. To be a person means to move on to the next experience.

Among people with terminal illness, those are happiest who are busy and productive. Breast-beating and screaming may offer some temporary relief, but any life to be worthwhile must be lived in the NOW mood and mode.

Religion and You

In a recent survey, it was pointed out that 75 percent of all college students believe in a God who judges us. This means that if you have faith, you are not in the minority. We may not always agree with God's judgment of us. When death comes, we may feel that God did not administer justice. Instead of blaming God or ourselves, we should try to understand that death is a mystery. We can understand the "cause" of death: it can be illness, accident, or through deliberate intent. The "why" may never be known.

It does little good just to sit and wonder. Life is full of "why's." Our task, as I see it, is to learn from religion and find the strength to go forward. We comfort the mourners. Then we must continue along the pathway of experience. You will learn from whatever comes your way. Death itself may be the greatest teacher. You will learn of people's true feelings. You will see how they act under stress. And, above all else, you will gain some insight into the essential nobility of persons. Most are able to cope with the death of a loved one. Families often close ranks and become strong again.

Our task is to be there when our friends need us. Even if you say nothing, just to be with them, in their home, in their time of need—often this is enough.

Thought Questions

1. How do you feel about living in a world where God permits death to occur?

2. Would people be more religious if science were one day able to overcome death?
3. Do you believe there is a heaven and a hell?
4. Does science tend to make people less religious?
5. Do you think a person has a soul that lives on after death?
6. Have you ever discussed your feelings about death with your clergyperson?
7. How can religion help us face the problem of death?

CHAPTER XI

Conclusions

On the morning of January 17, 1977, at Point of the Mountain, Utah, Gary Gilmore was executed by a firing squad. He said he was sorry for his crimes. His last words were, "Let's do it." The death of Gilmore ended a ten-year moratorium on the death penalty in America. It reflected a change in the mood of many people. Polls show that a majority in America do favor the death penalty. What made the Gilmore case fascinating was the desire of the convicted murderer to die. He wanted to be put to death. He willed parts of his body to science. He willed funds that might accrue from motion-picture, television, and book publication rights to the families of his victims. Strenuous efforts were made by civil-rights and other anti-death-penalty groups to prevent his execution. Ultimately, Gilmore was granted his wish.

His death was a further extension of the controversy over the question of who controls your life—and your death. As a person, do you have the right to die—by a firing squad, by mercy killing, or by suicide? Society is mobilized on the side of keeping you alive. In Gilmore's case, he was not put to death until after he had made two suicide attempts, and after making strenuous appeals to the court pleading to be executed. Even then, others appealed for a stay of execution. Some sought to have him pardoned, saying that he had suffered enough. Gilmore preferred death to life imprisonment. At one point he said that he did not deserve to live. Should this choice have been his—or was society to make the decision?

Gilmore's death was to spread the case of capital punishment across the front pages of the newspapers. His death will not still the debate. Others who wait in cells on Death Row felt that they were vitally affected. Gilmore's death could serve to hasten other executions. Once the ten-year moratorium is broken, other states will be emboldened also to execute convicted murderers.

CONCLUSION

Many states are now enacting new capital punishment laws. If the laws are drawn keeping the US Supreme Court decisions in mind, the death penalty is legal. The states must structure their laws so that the convicted criminal first is given every chance to prove his or her innocence.

An Ongoing Problem

The subject of death is as old as human experience. From the beginning of time, men have wondered about how they came to be upon this earth. And, having arrived here, they wondered what they were supposed to do. During man's long sojourn, he developed ideas as to his purpose for living. In Old Testament tradition, the Ten Commandments became a basic guide, part of a moral code of conduct. Through trial and error, men wrote great sacred books. Religions evolved that were to explain and justify man's conduct. They were based on man's experience in the world and his intuitive feeling that a Supreme Power was guiding his destiny. Experience showed him that he would not survive if he killed his neighbor, so he brought forth the law: Thou shalt not kill. Yet he saw that people did die. Even though you were not slain in battle, you still had a limited number of years.

Death was part of the reality of the human condition. Much of primitive man's time was spent in fighting against death. He killed animals and ate them so as to stay alive. He built a fire in his cave so that the cold would not cause him to freeze to death. He wore animal skins to protect him from the elements. But he knew that eventually, as the Indians said, he would go to the "happy hunting grounds" beyond the lake and forest. Primitive man looked to the sky. There he saw the sun, moon, and stars. Gentle rain gave him life-giving water. The world could be a friendly place at one moment, or very hostile the next.

Our earliest ancestors found that most of their time was consumed in hunting, fishing, and trapping. They exhausted themselves in acquiring enough food to sustain life. Painfully, over thousands of years, man has evolved. His brain has grown larger. No longer must he spend all his waking hours in the struggle to survive. He now has some leisure. He can think, meditate, read, watch television, or listen to radio and tapes. He lives in a multimedia world that brings far-off events into his living room. He no longer exhausts himself to obtain the basics of food, clothing, and shelter. Now, he can think. Theologians and philosophers have written great books about the meaning of life. He wonders, "What is life all about? Why am I here? What should I do? Where will I go after I die?"

As man's technological prowess increased, he began to think of himself as the center of the universe. Even the Bible said that God gave him dominion over all the animals of the earth. The more science revealed, the less able was man to accept the idea of an all-powerful God. If man is the center of everything, then who needs God? At the same time, he had many unanswered questions. For every answer that science gave, many new questions were raised. For example, science gave us the insecticide DDT, but after a number of years nature developed insects that could resist DDT. After medicine found ways to prolong life, man was then faced with the question—at what point do you allow a person to die with dignity? So, for every advance, a new problem arose.

If man is the center of everything, then he should have solutions. A scientific age says that there are answers if we probe deeply. Through the miracle of research, a human heart can be transplanted. Marvelous machines can keep a kidney functioning. Many parts of the body can be transferred from one person to another. Soon man was faced with such problems as who shall live and who shall die? For example, if a hospital ward has only so many dialysis machines, who shall be given the use of them? Decisions were faced. Shall a heart transplant be given to patient A or B? Who is most worthy of being saved? Science went beyond man's wildest dreams. Was science the handmaiden of man, or its enemy? Did science destroy faith, or enhance it? After all, the clergy go to the doctors when they are sick. Science and religion were not at war, but science did seem to negate religion. Some decided that science was God and would provide all of the answers. Others felt that moral decisions were still in the realm of religious truth.

The Right to Life

What of the rights of the fetus? With abortion techniques perfected by medicine, does religion have anything to say about bringing a child into the world? Here is a situation where religions clash. Some religionists say that to kill a fetus is to kill a life. Other clergypersons say that the soul does not enter the fetus until it emerges from the womb, so abortion should be permissible. The debates on this issue have not abated.

Science and religion often are in conflict. Science can provide techniques to save life (heart operations) or destroy it (atomic weapons). How shall the gifts of science be used? What is morally right or morally repulsive? Again, we seem to be moving into the arena of open choice. Neither science nor religion has absolute truth. Everything is up for discussion, be it heart transplants, abortion, or mercy killing.

My Right to Die?

Do the Gary Gilmores have the right to demand their own execution? Should a person suffering from a terminal illness have the right to demand an overdose of morphine to end his pain once and for all? Should a deeply troubled individual have the right to take his own life? Does our life belong to us, or to society? Individual rights and the will of society can be in conflict. The issues become very complex. Often they are bogged down in legal doubletalk. The more complex the society, the more difficult are the choices we face. No decision is simple. What are the human rights we should enjoy? What criteria can we use to determine what is really correct? There are many more questions than answers. And, whatever decision is made, many will still have guilt feelings.

To Die Alone

It sometimes happens that a dying patient rejects you, after you have visited her many, many times. As death approaches, the patient may be slowly detaching herself from family and friends. She now wants some quiet moments with her own thoughts. Psychologically this can be a healthy desire. Not every dying person wants a deathbed scene, surrounded by dear ones. In growing up, it is a sign of maturity to create a distance between yourself and your parents, showing that you are attaining independence. In like manner, the dying person may be showing wisdom in creating space between herself and her family. She has said all that needs to be said. The ultimate acceptance of death is to be hers alone. In every other situation, we can face problems with the help and support of others; but for our final moments on earth, we may wish to detach ourselves from the living, since we are entering into another stage of experience. It may be that the dying patient envisions starting out on a long journey, in which loved ones cannot be with her. Thus, if the patient refuses to see you, it is not a sign of displeasure. Perhaps everything that could be said and done has been accomplished, and detachment from life has set in. Doctors and nurses have spoken of this unusual phenomenon. It is the better part of wisdom to accede to the patient's wishes. Sister Mary Ellen Burke pointed out this tendency, based on her hospital work as a counselor to the dying. She was giving a lecture to a class in Pastoral Counseling that I attended at the Post Graduate Center for Mental Health in New York City on a recent day. Others in the class spoke of having similar experiences while bringing comfort to the dying. It is vital to be with the patient when you are wanted and needed. At the same time, we must respect a dying person's desire for privacy.

Death's Place

The human mind is free. Each day of your life, something pertaining to death will present itself. The young adult who matures at a normal pace learns to take everything in stride. Death has a place in the scheme of human experience. When it comes, it is, in truth, probably the last experience—certainly the final moment—that we will share with others on this earth. Our main concern is with life, and comforting those who have sustained the loss of a loved one. Death should not dominate life. A philosopher has said, "'Live every day as if it will be your last day on this earth." He sought to inspire his readers to regard time as very precious. However, I would question the wisdom of this quotation. Do not submit to undue pressure each day. In my opinion, to live with the notion that today may be the last day on earth is to distort reality.

As a young person, you do not see death as a friend—unless you visit one of your peers who is dying a painful death from an incurable disease. If you see this, then you may draw the painful conclusion that death is not always the enemy: it can bring relief, and eternal rest.

If we had the wisdom to live decently and productively, we might develop the maturity to approach death on a more rational basis. However, death does challenge our normal defenses. Even the most brilliant of us give way to unaccountable feelings. Dr. Kubler-Ross and others do show us some guidelines as to what our reactions might be. Still, in the final analysis, your reaction to death is very subjective. It has to do, primarily, with your own feelings and attitudes.

There is no adequate way to prepare yourself for the loss of a loved one. The most that you can do—when it occurs—is to ventilate your emotions, share your grief with others, and then emerge from your period of mourning with a renewed desire to live a useful life. If your role is to comfort a friend who mourns, then it is vital to be there and, by your presence, be able to show both in your words and in your silence that you truly care.

Thought Questions

1. Should a person on Death Row have the right to demand his or her own death?
2. How do you feel about euthanasia?
3. Should artificial means ever be used to keep a patient alive?
4. What is your reaction to the current abortion laws?
5. How can we best show mourners that we really care about them?
6. Would the world be better if people lived forever?

Bibliography

Aries, Philippe. *Western Attitudes Toward Death*. Maryland: Johns Hopkins University Press, 1974.

Caine, Lynn. *Widow*. New York: William Morrow and Company, Inc., 1974.

Choron, Jacques. *Death and Western Thought*. New York: Macmillan, 1963.

Durkheim, Emil. *Suicide* (1897), trans. J. A. Spaulding and G. Simpson. New York: Free Press, 1951.

Ice, J. L., and Carey, J. L. *The Death of God Debate*. Philadelphia: Westminster Press, 1967.

Kubler-Ross, Elisabeth. *On Death and Dying*. New York: Macmillan, 1969.

McLuhan, Marshall, and Fiore, Quentin. *The Medium Is the Message*. New York: Random House, 1967.

Murchland, Bernard. *The Meaning of the Death of God*. New York: Random House, 1967.

Tofler, Alvin. *Future Shock*. New York: Random House, 1970.

Index

A
abortion, 65, 128
acceptance
 of death, 48, 50
 need for, 32
aged needs of, 57, 58
aging, 52-61
 disability of, 83
 fight against, 20-21
aggressor, male v. female, 33-34
AIDS (acquired immunodeficiency syndrome), 38, 110-113
altruistic suicide, 29, 39
anger, 38
 child's, 98, 100, 102
 at death, 44, 45, 47, 49, 80, 83, 89, 115
anomic suicide, 29-30
Aries, Philippe, 81
autism, 31

B
bargaining, with God, 45-47, 49
Beck, Ernest, 81
Beebe, Hank, 59
Belushi, John, 37
Bias, Len, 28
birthrate, 55
blood transfusion, 111
body language, 97, 104, 105
body, viewing of, 76-77
Bowlby, John, 101
Brown, Edmund G. Jr., 71-72
burial
 customs, 84, 114
 society, 74
Burke, Mary Ellen, 130

C
Caine, Lynn, 44, 107
cancer, coping with, 85-96
capital punishment, 126
casket, 73, 74, 75, 76
change, age of, 30-32, 35, 53
children
 and death, 97-109
 and funerals, 21, 98, 102-103

choice, power of, 64
Christianity, 118
Christian Science, 47
clergy
 anger at, 46
 consulting, 19, 40, 44, 48, 77, 105-106, 114
 and living will, 70
 role of, 115-116
coma, 19, 64, 66
communication
 improving, 17
 interpersonal, 105
 overload, 32
counselor
 AIDS, 111, 112
 college, 27
 dying, 80, 83, 130
 professional, 47
courage, 95-96
cremation, 65, 73, 84
crime rate, 31-32
crying
 at funeral, 35
 for grief, 100, 101, 103
curiosity, about death, 82-84

D
death
 with dignity, 68, 69
 facing, 78-81, 106
 instinct, 28, 38, 40, 63
 as a process of life, 79-80
 rate, 20
denial, of death, 43-44, 47, 49, 102, 111, 112
Denial of Death, The, 81
depression, 25, 26, 37, 38, 43, 47-48, 78, 81, 111
diabetes, 88
drugs
 abuse of, 28, 37, 38, 110-111, 112
Durkheim, Émile, 21, 28, 29-30

E
ego, 40

133

egoistic suicide, 29
emotions, expressing, 100-101, 103, 122
empathy, 107, 109
escape, suicide as, 25, 38
euthanasia, 20, 67, 79, 72, 129

F
failure, 26, 30
faith
   in medicine, 70-71
   religious, 120
      loss of, 121, 123
fear
   of death, 23, 51, 66, 76, 83, 89
   of euthanasia, 68
   irrational, 87
   of old age, 55
   survivors', 80, 122
Federal Trade Commission, 75
Freud, Sigmund, 37, 40, 50, 119
frustration, 38, 39, 44, 46, 76, 79, 80, 83, 115
funeral, 47, 63
   costs of, 72-73, 81
   industry, 73-84
   teenager's, 17
funeral director, 73, 74, 75, 76, 78
Future Shock, 30

G
gang, joining, 32, 34
Gilmore, Gary Mark, 65, 126
God
   anger at, 44
   questions about, 116-117, 128
grandparents, 52, 54, 57-58, 59-60, 79
   foster-, 58, 59
grief, 17, 47
   excessive, 78
   working out, 48, 76, 93, 98, 100, 101, 103, 105
guilt feelings
   about atomic bomb, 23
   about dead person, 45, 48, 76, 102
   about dying, 90
   about living will, 68
   of survivors, 77-78, 79, 83, 89, 115

H
heart disease, 87, 88
helplessness, 17-18, 44, 45, 67

Heyer, Hill, 59
Hodgkin's disease, 89
homosexual, 34, 38, 110
hotline, suicide, 40

I
id, 37, 40
idealism, 39
illness
   chronic, 55-56
   incurable, 88
   terminal, 64, 66
instability, 30-31

J
Judaism, 76

K
Kelly, Orville, 87, 89
Kennedy, John F., 19, 21, 50
Kennedy, Robert, 19
King, Martin Luther Jr., 19
Klinghofer, Leon, 21
Kubler-Ross, Elisabeth, 44, 48-49, 50, 79, 131
leukemia, 89, 111
life
   after death, 50-51, 117-118, 119-120
   detachment from, 129-130
   expectancy, 55, 88-89
   right to, 128-129
living will, 19, 62-72
Lonely Crowd, The, 31
love
   absence of, 37
   need for, 54, 103, 104, 105

M
machine, life-sustaining, 18-19, 46, 68, 69, 79, 128
Make Today Count, 87-96
malpractice suit, 46, 67
Malthus, Thomas R., 55
maturity, reaching, 108-109
McLuhan, Marshall, 19, 30
Media Is the Message, The, 19
melanoma, 89
Messiah complex, 41, 77
mourning
   end to, 106, 124
   home in, 18, 47, 97

INDEX

N
National Funeral Directors Association, 74
nuclear family, 53
nursing home, 20, 58

P
pardon, buying God's, 45
parents, independence of, 54-55
past, retreat into, 49-50
permissiveness, 36
prayer, 45
  answer to, 46
  for dead, 121-122
pressure, sexual, 35

Q
Quinlan, Karen Ann, 18-19

R
Reagan, Ronald, 20
reality
  of death, 63-64, 127
  defense against, 43, 45, 47
  losing touch with, 25, 31
religion
  and cancer, 90
  and death, 46, 114-121
  and suicide, 38
responsibility, 38
  moral, 68, 69
retirement, 56
  age of, 20-21, 52
  compulsory, 53
Riesman, David, 31
role model, male, 32, 34
role strain, 35-36
Roman Catholic Church, 117
roots, family, 31, 60

S
safe sex, 110, 112, 113
self
  sense of, 36
  trust in, 106-108

self-esteem, loss of, 36
self-image, 37, 39
self-punishment, suicide as, 27
situation ethics, 38-39
society
  matriarchal, 32
  sick, 30
  "throw-away," 30
stress, living with, 32-33
success
  drive for, 27
  instant, 30
  pressure for, 25
  society geared to, 34
suicide
  of elderly, 54
  pacts, 25
  prevention, 38
  talking about, 37, 56, 90
  teenage, 25-41, 80
  tendency to, 48, 111
superego, 40, 119
support, for survivors, 104, 107

T
taboos, about death, 19, 21
television, impact of, 19-20, 30, 36
terrorism, 21
thanatology, 20
Tofler, Alvin, 30-31
Truman, Harry S., 23, 50
truth, telling to patient, 86-88

U
unconscious, 23, 40

W
Widow, 44, 107
women, suicide among, 33
women's liberation, 35
work ethic, 20, 36, 52